DISCARD

Praise for *The Leaderful FieldBook*

"*The Leaderful Fieldbook* provides real-life, pragmatic approaches to practicing personal and organizational change through assessments, case study, team tools, organizational design practices, consultative and communication models, skill/competency building, and much more. This is a book that will be actively used by practitioners, consultants, executives, students, and managers from organizations of all sizes and geographies for many years to come."

—Louis Carter, founder and CEO, Best Practice Institute

"This book will be a wonderful reference for the experienced practitioner or executive and an invaluable guide for the newcomer to the field of leadership development. In this highly actionable set of tools and stories, Joe Raelin and his colleagues have captured a lifetime of insights about what really makes a difference in leadership."

—T.J. Elliott, chief learning officer, vice president, Strategic Workforce Solutions, Educational Testing Service

"Offered here is a model of how an inclusive and engaging process of leadership can happen."

—Stephen Billett, professor, Griffith University, Australia

"Joe Raelin has long been *the* expert in understanding the theories and principles of the new leadership that incorporates concurrence, collectiveness, collaboration, and compassion. *The Leaderful Fieldbook* provides the insights and strategies that will allow each one of us to become a better leader as well as develop others to become great leaders."

— Michael Marquardt, president, World Institute for Action Learning, and author of *Leading with Questions* and *Optimizing the Power of Action Learning*

"Joe Raelin has artfully bundled centuries of combined experience by the world's leadership experts into one accessible guidebook. This is a powerful book!"

on Haggerty, EdD, associate provost, graduate studies, Champlain College

I0899358

"Now that the heroic leader idea is dead, the search is on to find ways of engaging as many members of organizations as possible in collaborative forms of leadership practice. This book, whose author is passionate about the need to realize democratic principles in organizations, helps meet that need. With its focus on five integrated levels of change, Joe Raelin's text is bursting with useful suggestions for adoption or adaptation by coaches, facilitators, developers, and network 'weavers.' *The Leaderful Fieldbook* provides a clearly articulated, highly accessible and useful exposition in which there are numerous practical activities for the improvement of personal performance and organizational betterment."

—Peter Gronn, professor, University of Cambridge

"Just as *Creating Leaderful Organizations* set out the tapestry of modern leadership, *The Leaderful Fieldbook* provides the threads for weaving it into everyday practice. Here we have a wealth of practical interventions, from up-to-the-minute activities to classic inventories. Raelin creatively, almost playfully, juxtaposes the cognitive and the experiential, the serious and the fun, the graphic and the rational, the intuitive and the systematic. The overall feel of this book is energizing and engaging. Any change agent—whether coach, facilitator, networker, or consultant—will find here a rich resource for leaderful practice."

**—Chris Mabey, director, Centre for Leadership
at University of Birmingham, UK**

THE
Leaderful
FIELDBOOK

STRATEGIES AND ACTIVITIES FOR DEVELOPING
LEADERSHIP IN EVERYONE

JOSEPH A. RAELIN

DAVIES-BLACK
an imprint of Nicholas Brealey Publishing

BOSTON • LONDON

First published by Davies-Black, an imprint of Nicholas Brealey Publishing, in 2010.

20 Park Plaza, Suite 1115A
Boston, MA 02116, USA
Tel: + 617-523-3801
Fax: + 617-523-3708

3-5 Spafield Street, Clerkenwell
London, EC1R 4QB, UK
Tel: +44-(0)-207-239-0360
Fax: +44-(0)-207-239-0370

www.nicholasbrealey.com

Printed in the United States of America.

14 13 12 11 10   1 2 3 4 5

ISBN: 978-0-89106-380-3

Library of Congress Cataloging-in-Publication Data

Raelin, Joseph A., 1948–
   The leaderful fieldbook : strategies and activities for developing leadership in everyone / Joseph A. Raelin.
      p. cm.
   Includes bibliographical references and index.
   ISBN 978-0-89106-380-3 (alk. paper)
  1. Executive coaching. 2. Leadership. I. Title.
   HD30.4.R32 2010
   658.4'092--dc22

2010008495

Contents

List of Activities & Cases

LIST OF ACTIVITIES

LIST OF CASES

Foreword

IN MY CAREER, I'VE WORN THE VARIOUS HATS of coach, facilitator, OD consultant, and weaver that Joe Raelin describes in this book—sometimes all in one day! But I haven't always had the language or logic to describe them or the ability to explain why I would be playing in those capacities. It's nice to have a set of concepts, labels, strategies, tools, and activities all in one place, so I can finally tell my parents, "See, this is what I do!"

But more importantly, this is a comprehensive fieldbook that can serve a community of practitioners and become a platform for professional collaboration in what can often be a lonely role.

The great thing about being a change agent on a mission to create a leaderful organization is that every action you take serves as an example for what could be. I say it's great because such clarity makes the decisions around "how" to behave in an organization easier to determine. More than a few times, I've found myself in embattled positions where I'd really like to grab control and ram a decision through so we can just move forward. Maybe that would be viewed as a courageous act of *leadership*, but that's the opposite of the *leaderful* thing to do.

Change of the sort Joe addresses in this book is not simple, easy, or fast. Leaderful transformations can take years to accomplish. The world seems to reward the short-term heroic efforts of leaders who "get stuff done," so the traditional model of leadership persists. And those who are successful in these short sprints defend their positions mightily. But look more closely, and the short-term gains are illusions of progress that often destroy long-term value. As soon as there is a peak in results, it is closely followed by a valley of losses. Leaders who "sell short" to impress investors usually fail in the long run as customers and employees get burned and move on to better situations.

Companies that understand the value of the long view are more likely to have leaderful tendencies. This is because their members have taken the time to identify and engage everyone affected by, or who cares about, the critical decisions within their community. Not to say that the leaderful approach is slow; it can be very fast when quick decisions are needed because, once established, all the key stakeholders are on board.

As agents of change, we face a real tension between the reliance on past models and a demand to move towards better circumstances. How do we shift from what feels like an addiction to short-term results to a more meaningful, sustainable organization that produces more value for the world? Like any other kind of addiction, it takes some serious commitment by a whole bunch of people to pull out of the old ways. Don't try to do it on your own.

In my most recent efforts as a change agent at IDEO, which is quite clearly a leaderful organization, I've really come to respect how difficult it is to facilitate change in organizations. The dominant mindset of traditional leadership is pervasive in the world of business and even creeps into such a place as IDEO. But, for the most part, if you were to observe our dozens of project teams in action, you would not be able to pick out a position leader in the bunch. IDEO has shown hundreds of times over that collaborative leadership is a very effective model for creating breakthrough results in very challenging circumstances.

Yet when faced with strategic organizational challenges, the starting point for IDEO is often the default of asking someone in charge for an answer. I believe this is due to the deficiency of "other" tools, processes, and structures available in the world that are built to the specifications of leaderful organizations, not traditional ones. And most senior players in today's world grew up with traditional education and traditional organizations as their training ground. Old habits die hard, even when they are surrounded with a culture and organization like we have at IDEO.

I believe that the dawn of the 21st Century is bringing a renaissance in organizational behavior, and new tools and processes are coming to life every day.

Still some of the "new" tools are aimed in the wrong direction, designed to prop up the one leader of a group, missing the possibility of engaging the full expertise of a leaderful community. How can we sort the new, effective tools from those that keep us locked in our old ways?

This is where Joe Raelin's book makes it mark. *The Leaderful Fieldbook* is a singular source of ideas and activities aimed at the five key levels of engagement necessary to shift completely to a new way of leading. Leadership is a systems challenge, not an individual development problem. For too long, leadership development has focused on the skills of the individual, when what is needed is a complete overhaul of the whole paradigm.

I've been working in this direction for most of my adult life—and I find many great ideas and resources in *The Leaderful Fieldbook*. It seems I spend much of my time at the individual and interpersonal levels of change work, helping others connect better. I'm a big fan of the "left hand column" as a tool to help people uncover their assumptions and create better alignment. And my more recent work has taken me deeper and deeper into the possibilities of great dialogue through more effective questioning. I've found that the best individual leaders ask more questions than those around them, and the "balancing advocacy with inquiry" framework is a great way to help people learn together.

If more people would take the time to use just one tool from each of the five levels of change outlined in this book, the results would be astounding. Taken individually they are each interesting and often produce a great moment, but taken as a set to be applied systematically at multiple layers in an organization, the whole is much greater than the sum of its parts. I urge you not to use this as a recipe book where you pick and choose an item to serve. Instead, use this as a script of activities you perform in a masterful effort toward leaderful transformation.

John Foster
Head of Talent and Organization
IDEO
Palo Alto, California
February 10, 2010

Introduction

THIS FIELDBOOK IS BASED ON THE PREMISE that leadership may be constituted as a democratic approach known as "leaderful" practice. Leaderful practice, in turn, is based on a fundamental humanistic principle that can be simply stated: When people who have a stake in a venture are given every chance to participate in and affect the venture, including its implementation, their commitment to the venture will be heightened. Democratic leadership, no matter what form it may take—participative management, total quality management, or organizational learning—requires full participation in leadership and decision making at all levels in the organization and in multiple decision processes.

The word *practice* in leaderful practice signifies that leadership need not be centered on the traits of any one individual but that we can find it in the everyday practice of those who are engaged. It is less about what one person thinks and does and more about what people do together to accomplish important activities. What makes the exchanges between people leaderful is their commitment to collaborate with one another to accomplish a shared purpose. They don't contribute to leadership sequentially, however, or one at a time; they do so all together and at the same time.

To fully appreciate the applications and possibilities of democratic leaderful practice, let's first review its contrast in what I might refer to as the traditional model of leadership.

The Traditional Model of Leadership

Most of us have grown up with this model. We can call it *implicit*, suggesting that its meaning is so widely accepted that there is no need to question its prevailing connotation. In other words, the qualities of traditional leadership have become commensurate with leadership itself. Here, then, are my nominations for the tenets that best describe the Western historical tradition of leadership.

1. *Leadership is serial.* Once one achieves an office of leadership, the leader retains that position at least for the duration of the term of office. Only when one completes his or her term, or vacates or is forced to leave the office, does leadership transfer to a successor. A leader is thus always in a position of leadership and does not cede the honor to anyone else unless his or her time is up. Indeed, once they have acquired power, most leaders attempt to sustain or increase it and not give it up.
2. *Leadership is individual.* Leadership is a solitary role. There is only one leader of an enterprise; normally this person is designated as the authority or the position leader. It weakens or, at a minimum, confuses leadership to have more than a single leader or to share leadership because no one, then, has the final say in making decisions and directing actions.
3. *Leadership is controlling.* The traditional leader believes that it is his or her ultimate duty to direct the enterprise and engender the commitment of all the employees of the organization. To ensure smooth coordination of functions, the leader is the spokesperson for the enterprise. The subordinate's role is to follow the guidance of the leader and to help him or her successfully accomplish the mission.
4. *Leadership is dispassionate.* Although the leader recognizes that people have feelings, the leader's function is to make the tough decisions for the enterprise in a dispassionate manner. Tough decisions may result in not satisfying (or may even hurt) stakeholders, including employees, but accomplishing the mission of the enterprise must come first. Leaders are the authoritative source when facing problems in the operation and tend to exude confidence that they are in charge and that subordinates can rely upon them to handle any challenge facing the enterprise.

A Brief History of the Traditional Model

The traditional model tends to paint the leader with heroic imagery. Where has this heroic paradigm come from? We can trace the concept of leadership back to its root. The Anglo-Saxon *lédan*—for leadership—has the meaning of "going forth" or "standing out in front." In the nineteenth century, Scottish historian Thomas Carlyle insisted that the one certainty that defines history is what "Great Men" have accomplished. Perhaps this is why the pull toward the heroic model of leadership persists even though there is much talk about the need to include other members of the organization under the leadership umbrella. Though the value of democratic leadership may be advocated, the drive to have a charismatic leader whom we can love and who can save us sneaks back into our consciousness just as we prepare to assert our own worth and independence. Part of the reason for this is that many Western cultures value individualism while preaching teamwork. Whatever the walk of life, be it a corporate setting, a sports team, or an opera, there tends to be a focus on the star performer even when he or she may be entirely dependent upon the team to achieve prominence.

The Leaderful Practice Model

Leaderful practice offers an alternative approach to the traditional model of leadership. Leaderful practice, as we shall discuss it, is characterized by four contrasting operating tenets known as the Four Cs. These Four Cs call on leaders to be concurrent, collective, collaborative, and compassionate (see Figure I.1).

The first tenet, that leaders be *concurrent*, stipulates that there can be more than one leader operating at the same time in an organization. Leaders willingly and naturally share power with others. Indeed, power can be increased when everyone works together. Since leaders carry a variety of responsibilities in an organization, it can be counterproductive to insist that there be only one leader operating at any one time and that this person stay in power until replaced serially by the next authority. For example, an administrative assistant who "knows the ropes" and can help people figure out who is knowledgeable about a particular function may be just as important to the group as the position leader. However, this same position leader does not "stand down" or give up his or her leadership as members of the group turn their attention to the administrative assistant. The two of them as well as many others can offer their leadership at the same time.

According to the second tenet, leaderful practice is *collective*. Since a group can have more than one leader operating at a time, people might operate as leaders together; in other words, leadership is a plural not just an individual phenomenon. The collective view purports that leadership does not derive from individual influence; rather it emanates from the

FIGURE **I.1**
The Four Cs of Leaderful Practice*

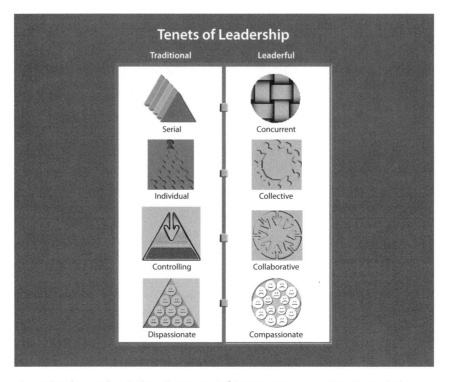

*Copyright © by Joseph A. Raelin in *Creating Leaderful Organizations: How to Bring Out Leadership in Everyone* (San Francisco: Berrett-Koehler, 2003).

process of people working together for a common purpose. According to this interpretation, anyone may rise to serve the group's leadership needs. The entity is not solely dependent on one individual to mobilize action or make decisions on behalf of others. I include in this assertion the role of the position leader. This "authority" may have formal power conferred on him or her by the organization, but formal authority is not necessarily the most valuable to the operation. Decisions are made by whoever has the relevant responsibility. Leadership may thus emerge from multiple members of the organization, especially when important issues arise, such as preparing for a strategic intervention, creating meaning for the group, or proposing a change in direction. Although someone may initiate an activity, others may become involved and share leadership with the initiator.

Consider a team temporarily stymied in its attempt to solve a problem. Feeling disconsolate, members wonder if they will ever find a solution. Suddenly, some member offers an idea, perhaps not a mainstream idea, but one that has an immediate appeal and engages everyone's imagination. Soon, others begin throwing out additional thoughts and tactics to build on the original idea. For a time, there is an almost breathless quality to the team's functioning as it becomes absorbed in this all-encompassing solution process. The team is experiencing collective leadership; it is not dependent on any one member, not the position leader, not the idea initiator; everyone is participating. Further, the collective nature of leadership illustrated here incorporates the critical components of learning and meaning making. Team members use their conversation to invent new ways to attack a problem and collectively make sense together from what once was a state of "not-knowing."

The third tenet posits that leaderful practice is *collaborative*. All members of the organization, not just the position leader, are in control of and may speak for the entire organization. They may advocate a point of view that they believe can contribute to the common good of the organization. Although they might be assertive at times, they are equally sensitive to the views and feelings of others and consider their viewpoints to be equally valid. They thus seek to engage in a public dialogue in which they willingly open their beliefs and values to the scrutiny of others. It is through dialogue that collaborative leaders co-create the enterprise. They also understand the difference between collaborating as a pretense versus becoming fully involved. In pretentious involvement, one quickly discovers that all the critical decisions seem to be made when one is absent. Collaborative leaders realize that everyone counts—every opinion and contribution sincerely matter.

Finally, leaderful managers are *compassionate*. By demonstrating compassion, one extends unadulterated commitment to preserving the dignity of others. Stakeholders' views are considered before making a decision for the entire enterprise. Rather than have one key individual make decisions dispassionately for the "good of the enterprise," each member of the organization is valued, regardless of his or her background or social standing, and all viewpoints are solicited whether or not they conform to current thought processes. In practicing compassion, leaders take the stance of a learner who sees the adaptability of the organization as dependent upon the contributions of others. Members of the organization, not necessarily the position leader, handle problems as they arise. Compassionate leaders recognize that values are intrinsically interconnected with leadership and that there is no higher value than democratic participation. The endowment of participation extends to the wider organization affected by the actions of a given stakeholder. If building a new corporate complex will affect the existing ecology or serenity of a neighboring property, the compassionate leader includes the neighbors in deliberations concerning the construction.

So, we have the ingredients for establishing a leaderful culture within the organization. Unfortunately, leaderful practice has not appeared in most Western cultures as the default option in exhibiting leadership. The individual heroic model still persists as the dominant approach. Consider a case, initially recounted by Dr. Richard Boyer,[1] of a hospital unit team. The members, having put up with a heavy-handed supervisor for fifteen years, got a chance to try out a self-directed approach when the supervisor left the hospital. They chose as their team leader someone who had highly developed interpersonal skills and who was considered to be a much kinder and gentler person. Originally, the team was excited about performing some of the administrative functions that had previously been handled by the former manager. The new team leader and the staff now worked alongside each other sharing administrative responsibilities. Over time, however, the team members began to push a lot of the shared responsibilities back onto the team leader. They reverted to their old ways and began to insist that the new team leader take on many of the responsibilities of the former manager. What happened to the self-directed team concept?

The case brings up the challenge of introducing leaderful practice when people and institutions aren't ready for it. Individuals and communities are not always standing by, primed to assume leaderful behavior. They need to evolve both an appreciation for and an ability to adopt leaderful practice. Although I advocate that individuals and institutions adopt a leaderful approach, I recognize that communities cannot become leaderful overnight.

Consequently, institutional change needs to be mobilized by internal or external change agents who can encourage the endorsement of a culture of learning and participation within the system in question. Change agency, in turn, needs to occur at multiple levels of experience: individual, inter-

---

[1] See the full case in M. Duncan Fisher and K. Fisher, "Leadership on Self-Managing Teams," *At Work*, May/June, 1998.

personal, team, organization, and network. Although members of a team or institution may be at a stage of readiness to assume leaderful properties, they may not choose to act without some provocation by those bold enough to take action. So in some instances, the change agent may only need to nudge others to act on their own and collectively; in other cases, the agent may need to mobilize a more dramatic change in outlook and behavior.

The Role of the Change Agent

Change agents develop their understanding of change processes conceptually from such disciplines as social psychology, organizational sociology, coaching, creativity, systems dynamics, organization development, strategy, and cultural anthropology. Veteran change agents also learn how to reflect upon and incorporate the lessons of experience into their change portfolios. They see every experience as an opportunity for learning and actively seek feedback from colleagues on how they might improve each engagement. They often develop their own style and professional identity, while bringing out the best in the client community, all of which allows for maximal creativity in the engagement.

Although it is to their advantage to have technical knowledge of the subject matter, leaderful change agents tend to focus on human dynamics, whether in the domain of personal development, interpersonal relations, team development, organizational learning, or social networks. They also tend to have effective communication skills, to display a high level of sensitivity, and to be authentic in their relations with others. Although most change agents can operate across multiple levels of change, it is also advisable for the change agent to know her or his strength so as not "to be all things to all people."

There are commonalities across the varying roles occupied by change agents working on behalf of leaderful development. A good place to start in identifying some of these roles is to consider the familiar management roles identified in Henry Mintzberg's work. In his book, *The Nature of Managerial Work*,[2] he explored three main roles: interpersonal, informational, and decisional. I previously suggested that interpersonal competencies are especially critical to the change agent, the reason being that these competencies invite learners to participate in their own personal and professional

---

[2] H. Mintzberg, *The Nature of Managerial Work* (New York: Harper & Row, 1973).

development or in the development of the institutions of which they are a part. The interpersonal roles can entail very deep listening and empathizing and can also require an agent to broker connections among stakeholders. The informational roles cover the need to assemble, select, monitor, and disseminate information. At times, the change agent may need to serve as a spokesperson on behalf of a change and its underlying values, such as its humanistic roots. Last, the agent may need to carry out some decisional roles, focusing on exploring new opportunities, allocating resources, handling disturbances, and encouraging learners to practice what is preached in leaderful behavior—namely, involving the full community in making sound decisions with compassion and creativity.

The Change Agent of Leaderful Development

What makes the change agent of leaderful development unique is a commitment to learning that is sufficiently participant-directed that learners comprehend, by the agent's practices, that leadership is a shared mutual phenomenon. This kind of agency is thus oriented to the development of independent and interdependent behavior that encourages increased autonomy among learners. Malcolm Knowles[3] referred to this form of development as "andragogical," rather than pedagogical or teacher directed. Andragogy encourages learners to be more capable of accepting greater levels of responsibility for their own and others' actions and more reliable in their assessment of their own capacities and developmental needs. In andragogical practice, leaderful agents model such behaviors as tolerance of ambiguity, openness and frankness, patience and suspension of judgment, empathy and unconditional positive regard, and commitment to learning. Eventually, the learners themselves adopt some of these same behaviors, thus limiting the proactivity of the agent.

The leaderful change agent tends to rely on the learners themselves to "learn through" their own problems and provides resource suggestions and alternative framings as well as advice on "learning how to learn." This means that the agent may invite learners momentarily to think out of their contexts or frames of reference in order to challenge existing assumptions and beliefs.

---

[3] M. Knowles, *The Modern Practice of Adult Education: From Pedagogy to Andragogy*, 2nd ed. (Englewood Cliffs, NJ: Prentice Hall, 1980).

Although the leaderful change agent is thus typically less directive than other change agents might be, he or she makes occasional interventions to help instigate leaderful change in particular settings, such as in a team environment. John Heron[4] recommended six intervention strategies that are appropriate to consider:

1. *Prescriptive* interventions deliberately offer advice or counsel.
2. *Informative* interventions offer leads or ideas about how to proceed on a given matter, that is, where to find an appropriate resource to contribute to a project.
3. *Confronting* interventions directly challenge learners on such issues as their current process, evolving relationships with others, and restricted intellectual frameworks.
4. *Cathartic* interventions address emotional undercurrents and seek to release tension by, for example, promoting the expression of grief or anger.
5. *Catalytic* interventions provide a structure or framework to encourage the development of an idea or to remove a blockage by, for example, suggesting that a learner stop, reflect, and write down his or her thoughts or asking someone to role-play an individual with whom he or she is reporting to have difficulty.
6. *Supportive* interventions display care and attention and offer empathy.

Ultimately, the leaderful change agent, no matter the level in which he or she is operating, needs to encourage the endorsement of a form of learning that Ron Heifetz[5] has characterized as leadership without "easy answers." What this means is that the system in question cannot operate by subscribing to rhetoric that offers a neat, quick solution that provides an illusion of accomplishment. Tough problems require rigorous examination that can come about through learning; this brand of learning requires a level of collective consciousness that goes beyond attending to symptoms of a problem. Rather, learners need to be willing to examine the fundamental assumptions behind their reasoning, carrying it to a level that invites scrutiny

---

[4] J. Heron, *Six Category Intervention Analysis. Human Potential Research Project* (Guildford, UK: University of Surrey, 1989).

[5] See R. A. Heifetz, *Leadership Without Easy Answers* (Cambridge, MA: Harvard University Press, 1994).

of successive layers of the problem, leading to as close an examination as possible of its causal structure.

This process of learning is often painful in that it often does not afford a pat answer. It takes longer because alternatives are subjected to a collective examination that often involves conflicts among competing ideas. Leaderful change agents are unusual in their willingness to subject their assumptions to public scrutiny. They are willing to face their own vulnerability that they may lose control, that their initial suppositions may turn out wrong, or that no solution may be found, at least in the short term.

Even more, these change agents are willing to face the utter reality that they themselves may not know the answer and that such a revelation to others, especially to their colleagues, might suggest their incompetence, not to mention their own fear of not knowing. What is key to learning is to transform the attribution of incompetence in not knowing the answer to that of competence in one's capacity to learn. Learning does not have to always reside in the expert or in any presumed "leader." Learning is a mobile, continuous, and collective process. Relying on any one person to produce it can make it stale. We need to uplift the value of inquiry in our lives. The person with the question should be admired as much as the person with the answer. No one needs to feel incompetent for not knowing the answer. Incompetence to the leaderful change agent is when an individual does not have the courage to look for the answer.

How does the leaderful change agent operate? Does he or she teach these attributes of learning? In what kind of setting? Clearly, the competencies embedded in performing a reflective or learning-to-learn response are not readily available from classroom training. It cannot be a matter of attending an off-site to learn the "list" of leadership skills. It is not the skills that count as much as the principles attending to the acquisition of learning competencies. In this sense, the skills are metacompetencies that address how one might learn in the midst of experience. So, in the instance of leadership, it is not a question of bringing people to leadership training as much as it is bringing leadership to the group so that everyone can participate in the practice of leadership.

In bringing leadership to the group, I am privileging the process of engagement as a basis for learning. But it is not only engagement that can create leaderful practice; it is just as critical that there be both private and collective reflection on the experience. Private reflection can be accomplished through planned and unplanned introspective processes, such as in using a journal. Collective or public reflection is accomplished in dialogue with others about real-time experience and is probably best pursued through the vehicle of the learning team. Learning teams assemble co-learners committed to helping each other learn and represent a vehicle that, along with journals, I will refer to liberally throughout this fieldbook. Leaderful change agents are encouraged to reinforce collective processes of learning by their learners consistent with leaderful practice, which happens to also constitute a collective process of leadership.

Overview of the Fieldbook

This fieldbook comes out of the "training of trainers" tradition as a resource to help agents in their own work with clients, by themselves or as members of other systems, whether small groups or larger networks. It embraces an experiential rather than a classroom pedagogy. Change agents, like most adult learners, learn best when they can reflect on real-life experiences going on within their own or their clients' work settings. They also like to learn with others and often prefer to learn at their own pace. With this fieldbook, they can also "live the learning," that is, apply it when it is most needed.

Thus, the approach used can be characterized as a form of work-based learning that seeks to integrate theory with practice and knowledge with experience. Its principles are simple. It sees learning as:

- Acquired in the midst of action and dedicated to the task at hand
- Collective, so that learning can become everyone's job
- Demonstrating a learning-to-learn aptitude freeing participants to search for fresh questions rather than rely on expert knowledge

Learning can be accomplished, then, just-in-time and in the right dose to be helpful to practice. Furthermore, it does not have to become disassociated from the notion of place. It can be designed to help change agents navigate their own interventions more effectively.

The final outcome from a leaderful intervention is a system in which everyone makes it their business to learn continuously and collectively as part of their everyday experience. They work incessantly to create an environment in which knowledge is freely exchanged. Their communities are characterized as learning cultures in which everyone becomes a partner in creating and expanding the sources of knowledge. As knowledge is adapted and enriched in this way, it transforms into learning. Embedded in a learning culture is the practice of reflection in which learners extend

TABLE **I.1**

Leaderful Agents of Change By Level

Level	Agent
Individual	Coach
Interpersonal	
Team	Facilitator
Organization	OD Consultant
Network	Weaver

time to their colleagues—to listen to them and to suspend their own beliefs during precious moments of empathy. The reflective orientation exhibited by leaderful participants also entails open-hearted acceptance, as community members treat one another as family members.

This fieldbook provides change agents with a series of strategies, activities, and cases at five levels of change: individual, interpersonal, team, organization, and network. I am also proposing here that the name designated for the change agent vary according to the level in question. Thus, as seen in Table I.1, the change agent at the individual and interpersonal levels is referred to as the *coach*; at the team level, the *facilitator*; at the organizational level, the *OD consultant*; and at the network level, the *weaver*.

STRATEGIES AND ACTIVITIES

Each chapter begins with an overview of change agency at the respective level. The activities for that level of change are then listed, followed by a detailed set of instructions to help the leaderful agent guide clients and colleagues through the activities. The description of each activity begins with a strategic overview providing a background and a purpose to the activity and linking it to its corresponding level of change.

A few of the activities in the fieldbook are designed to help the change agent reflect on his or her intervention plans privately or with a colleague. Most of the activities, however, represent a specific intervention to engage in and then reflect upon with a client group of learners. Aside from those recommended by my own colleagues, I have experimented with nearly all of the activities and, in some cases, have applied them over and over again in my teaching and consulting experience. Thus, they are tried and true and should practically run themselves.

CASE STUDIES

At the conclusion of each chapter, I include a fairly detailed case exemplifying one of the activities covered in the chapter. The cases, except for the one in chapter 3, which I prepared, have been written by my most respected colleagues in the field of social change. Each of these writers is, in my view, an expert in the level of change characterized in the respective chapter. Further, each has worked in depth with at least one of the activities in that chapter, constituting, as we know, the individual, interpersonal, organizational, or network level. Readers will note a degree of stylistic symmetry in the cases, since each of the writers was asked to prepare their case adhering to some broad guidelines—namely, that the case incorporate an introduction to the setting and characters, and that the authors cite:

- Why they chose to use the activity in question
- What they hoped to accomplish by using it
- How it worked out, and
- Why they felt the activity achieved the specific outcome of democratizing their client's practice

It is my hope that these cases add a degree of real-life vitality to the activities described in this fieldbook.

Use of the Fieldbook

As suggested earlier, most change agents operate at different levels, so readers may choose to skip around to experiment with some of the activities at their respective levels. However, if you're a specialist or are working currently with one of the specific levels, you would be advised to concentrate on a given chapter. Taken together, the fieldbook provides a comprehensive account of a set of applied activities and associated cases to promote the acquisition of leaderful practices in most institutional settings.

Readers may find it useful to read the full text on the theory and background of leaderful practice by consulting my book, *Creating Leaderful*

Organizations: How to Bring Out Leadership in Everyone.[6] This book provides a conceptual foundation for many of the activities featured in this fieldbook.

Although these applied activities are primarily designed for practitioners serving as change agents in the field, they can also be used by instructors in the areas of organization development, learning, and change who are working with experienced students. They can also be used by individuals who are committed to a process of self-development in leadership. These strategies, however, can only go so far. Any value will ensue from the reader's commitment to try them, reflect upon them, and learn from them.

---

[6] J. A. Raelin, *Creating Leaderful Organizations: How to Bring Out Leadership in Everyone* (San Francisco: Berrett-Koehler, 2003).

1

Individual-Level Change

THE PREMISE OF STARTING AT THE INDIVIDUAL LEVEL is that self-leadership skills are typically necessary before teams or organizations acquire the readiness for democratic leadership. One must become comfortable first in his or her own inner world and aware of his or her capabilities. When undertaking a process of self-discovery, we need to appreciate the mixture of life experiences that have led to our present way of being. Many of us need to find an inner purpose to guide our everyday activities. Others need to become more aware of the gap between our intentions and our behavior. This requires both an ability and a willingness to retrace our reasoning and the behavioral steps that have led to our actions. It requires the courage not only to examine ourselves independently but also to open our experiences to trusted others.

The work of the coach is to help individuals disclose in private to themselves and in conversation with others who they are and what meaning they bring to the world and to themselves. Coaching thus stems from its practice as a medium for reflection and learning. The parties—coach and learner—commit to exploring the social, political, and emotional reactions that might be blocking an individual's operating effectiveness. Otherwise confidential issues—such as working relationships with other colleagues, strategic business issues, or the participant's own growth and development—are given a forum for open consideration. Individuals get a rare opportunity to think out loud and receive constructive feedback on critical and even undiscussable problems.

The six activities in this chapter are designed to help change agents use and improve upon their coaching skills to work with learners to discover their inner selves.

The first activity, **Setting My Personal Learning Goals**, will help learners acquire a set of challenging development goals for mastering self-leadership as a first step in developing leaderful behavior.

The second activity, **Completing the Leaderful Questionnaire**, will help learners develop a baseline for their current views about leaderful practice. They score themselves on the "leaderful questionnaire" and are then invited to reflect on their scores with their coaches and mentors.

The third activity, **Draw-a-Horse**, extends beyond learners' perceptions of leaderful practice by engaging them in a simulation invoking potential leaderful behavior.

The fourth activity, **Squash**, gives learners an opportunity to detect their initial mindset about the meaning of leadership by reflecting on a decision they would make in a power-dependent scenario called "Squash."

The fifth activity, **Group Citizenship Behavior**, assesses the learner's citizenship behavior as it relates to his or her commitment to a group or team.

The sixth activity, **The Nine Shapes**, gives learners a chance to slow down and reflect on a pressing issue by examining it from multiple perspectives.

Personal Learning Goals

Personal learning goals constitute one way to conduct an initial examination of those elements of one's life that infuse it with meaning or accomplishment. In this activity, coaches work with clients and colleagues to produce a set of meaningful goals that capture the client's hopes and aspirations for personal self-discovery. Often, a goal concerns a change in some personal circumstances or requires rearranging a situation to be more aligned with one's intentions.

The development of personal learning goals is an evolving process. The learner's first goals may be superficial, reflecting others' expectations or representing aspirations already being accomplished. Over time and with the assistance of a coach and of significant others, the learner can learn to set more challenging goals that may profoundly strike at the heart of what really matters—what can truly motivate him or her to reach for deeper commitments.

The first activity is designed to help learners develop such goals and master self-leadership, a key step in the development of leaderful behavior.

....

ACTIVITY 1.1

Setting My Personal Learning Goals

The steps in this activity help gradually narrow the selection of meaningful goals, leading ultimately to the preparation of an individual development plan to create ongoing dialogue between the learner and coach or between the learner and others, both in the work environment and elsewhere, who are committed to the learner's leaderful development.

STEP 1: The first set of questions is designed to establish the context for goal development. Before working explicitly on any goals, learners should be encouraged to reflect on the conditions that prepare them most auspiciously for learning:

1. In what circumstances do you learn best:
    - By doing and taking action?
    - By talking out loud with others?
    - By listening?
    - By getting feedback from others?
    - By reading?
    - By surfing the Web?
    - By observing others?
2. What projects or experiences provide you with the greatest opportunity to learn?
3. The concept of a *learning style*, popularized by the work of Peter Honey and Alan Mumford[7] and in particular their Learning Styles Questionnaire, refers

---

[7] P. Honey and A. Mumford, *Capitalizing on Your Learning Style* (King of Prussia, PA: Organization Design and Development, 1989).

to one's preferences in the way to approach learning. What learning style do you tend to use to predispose you to maximal learning? Are you an

- *Activist:* You are inclined to involve yourself fully in new experiences and are willing to try anything once.
- *Reflector:* You like to stand back and ponder experiences, observing them from different perspectives.
- *Theorist:* You prefer to work with logic, concepts, and theory, often using a step-by-step approach, asking if things make sense.
- *Pragmatist:* You're interested in trying out ideas to see if they work, thus you tend to act fast and move from one thing to the next.

4. How might you change your script or use role reversal to try a new way to learn? For example, if you tend to use logic to work through most problems, consider examining your feelings or values as a basis to formulate your next decision and examine any differences from what would have been derived from the theoretical perspective.

5. In order to make room for more learning, consider these classic questions:
   - What will you stop doing?
   - What will you keep doing?
   - What will you do differently?
   - What will you start doing?

STEP 2: The next set of questions helps learners orient their goal development and, in so doing, will help them select the most challenging and useful goals.

1. Which goals will stretch you the most?
2. Which goals will help you confront your immediate personal, professional, and career challenges?
3. Which goals will take you most out of your comfort zone?
4. Which goals might help you overcome patterns that have interfered in the past with your work and life satisfaction?
5. Which goals will help you increase a needed knowledge or skill area?
6. Can you name goals that are specific, measurable, challenging, and yet attainable?

STEP 3: Now select three to five specific development goals that you would like to work on. They should have personal, professional, and/or career relevance; for example: "I wish to become more sensitive to how I come across to other people, especially to reduce my proclivity to talk over others who wish to get a word in."

Using the Personal Development Plan prototype provided in Figure 1.1, list your goals and consider the strategies that can be used to accomplish each goal:

- *Experiential activities.* Reflect on some challenging experiences, work assignments, or projects that might broaden and stretch your goals. How might particular work tasks or projects allow you to try out new knowledge or behavior and expose you to new challenges, people, or ways of doing things?
- *Educational experiences.* Supplement your on-the-job activities with formal courses, readings, conferences, or other professional experiences to provide you with foundational and background information or with more advanced knowledge.
- *Feedback from significant others.* Consult not only with your coach but with others who possess the skills you wish to develop or who can reliably observe you and provide objective feedback on the development of your goal. Find opportunities to observe them. Interview them about their own successes and challenges. Share with them your development goals and periodically solicit their feedback on your attempts to accomplish them.

STEP 4: Incorporate metrics and timetables.

- *Metrics* represent specific criteria—quantitative and qualitative—to help you and your coach know whether your development goals are or have been achieved. They provide a gauge to accomplishment as well as a basis for feedback exchange. A quantitative metric may be the number of times a new behavior has emerged in one's communications repertoire. A qualitative metric may constitute the manner—such as through nonverbal expression—by which one augments one's listening acuity and sensitivity.
- *Timetables*, where appropriate, point to a target date when the respective goal (or stages of goal accomplishment) may be accomplished and suggest opportune times when coaching sessions may be called for.

Figure 1.1, the Personal Development Plan, lays out the aforementioned steps. The figure may also be adapted and entered in one's journal. Note that the first goal has been filled in as an example.

FIGURE **1.1**

Personal Development Plan

Name: _____   Date: _____

Goal #	Development Goal	Strategies to Accomplish Each Goal [Experiential Activities; Educational Experiences; Feedback from Significant Others]	Metrics	Timetable
1.	Reduce proclivity to talk over others	• Reveal the goal to members of my Delta project team as a personal goal • Ask for specific feedback after the fourth meeting • Observe Meredith in my dept. weekly meetings as a model of a good listener • Consult with my coach about suggestions to sustain my exuberance yet increase my sensitivity and also ask about my progress on this goal • Enroll in the Learning Consortium's course in Appreciative Inquiry • Read the book *The Art of Powerful Questions*, discuss it with my coach, and apply some of the recommended practices	1. Observe members of my project team and department to see if they respond to me differently and keep notes in my journal 2. Interview 6 members of my project team and department and ask for specific feedback on this goal 3. Ask my wife if she has observed any reduction in my interruptions of our friends in our conversations 4. Complete the AI course and read the 'Questions' book and produce some add'l activities for practice, to be noted in my journal and raised with my coach	• After two months • After four months • After three months • By May 1

(Continued on next page)

[Add your own goals, strategies, metrics, and timetables]

2.

3.

4.

5.

Leaderful Development

In Activity 1.2, learners are asked to complete the Leaderful Questionnaire to develop a baseline of where they stand on the four tenets of leaderful practice—the Four Cs—concurrent, collective, collaborative, and compassionate leadership. The questionnaire both quantitatively and visually measures one's tendencies toward either traditional leadership or leaderful practice and preferences in between.

The coach should let learners know that it is impractical to expect high scores on each of the Four Cs. However, lower scores might suggest areas for subsequent goal development, for journal reflection, and for dialogue with one's coach or learning team. Once a baseline score has been acquired, the learner should be encouraged to return to the questionnaire at a subsequent date to see if and where scores have changed over time, leading to further reflection and dialogue.

....

ACTIVITY 1.2

Completing the Leaderful Questionnaire

Turning to the questionnaire in Figure 1.2, please mark where you stand on the twelve leadership views presented, using the scale of 1 to 5. Circle the number 1 if you completely agree with the left endpoint, 5 if you completely agree with the right endpoint. Values 2 and 4 suggest you somewhat agree with the endpoints, and 3 would mean that you are in between or neutral. There is no correct answer; the questions merely attempt to characterize your leadership predispositions.

When you have completed each item on the Leaderful Questionnaire, score your answers using this scoring chart.

Scoring Chart

To compute a score for concurrent leadership, compute: $a + e + i =$ ____

To compute a score for collective leadership, compute: $b + f + j =$ ____

To compute a score for collaborative leadership, compute: $c + g + k =$ ____

To compute a score for compassionate leadership, compute: $d + h + l =$ ____

To derive a total leaderful score, add the four
components together: Total Score = ____

FIGURE **1.2**

The Leaderful Questionnaire*

a.	1 = Once you're a leader, you don't relinquish it to anybody else	1—2—3—4—5	5 = Once you're a leader, you share it with others who may also be leading at the same time
b.	1 = Leadership resides in one member of a group	1—2—3—4—5	5 = Many people within a group may operate as leaders
c.	1 = A leader's duty is to direct the operation	1—2—3—4—5	5 = The direction of an operation should arise from the entire group
d.	1 = A leader has to make the tough decisions for the enterprise first even if it hurts some stakeholders	1—2—3—4—5	5 = A leader will consider the dignity of the stakeholders first before making a decision for the enterprise
e.	1 = Once acquiring power, you attempt to sustain or increase it, not lose it	1—2—3—4—5	5 = Power is acquired and increased by everyone working together
f.	1 = Authority is the principal basis of power in leadership	1—2—3—4—5	5 = Power in leadership can come from many sources beyond authority
g.	1= A leader should speak for the entire group	1—2—3—4—5	5 = Subordinates should feel comfortable to speak for the entire group
h.	1 = The leader is the authoritative source when facing problems in the operation	1—2—3—4—5	5 = There is no one authoritative source in the group; all viewpoints must be considered when facing problems
i.	1 = Sharing power as a leader would be abdicating responsibility	1—2—3—4—5	5 = Sharing power as a leader is a natural and desirable activity
j.	1 = One person should ultimately make the decisions on behalf of others	1—2—3—4—5	5 = Decisions are made by whoever has the relevant responsibility
k.	1 = It is important to share your deepest beliefs with only your closest associates	1—2—3—4—5	5 = You should engage in a public dialogue that opens your deepest beliefs to the scrutiny of other group members
l.	1 = A leader's job is to assure subordinates that they can rely upon him/her to handle any problem	1—2—3—4—5	5 = A leader encourages subordinates, not himself or herself, to handle problems as they arise

You can draw interpretations for these scores for the individual components as well as for the total score.

For the individual components:

- If your scores are < 9, you are inclined toward traditional leadership.
- If your scores are > 9, you are inclined toward leaderful practice.

For the total score:

- If your score is < 36, you are inclined toward traditional leadership.
- If your score is > 36, you are inclined toward leaderful practice.

Leaderful Behavior

To determine learners' penchant to engage leaderfully, it is helpful to see how they perform in a simulation that calls for them to respond to a challenging yet amusing predicament that entails collaborating with others. The simulation is called "Draw-a-Horse." The prior activity, involving the leaderful questionnaire, assessed the learner's perception of how he or she views leadership, but it was not a behavioral measure. The Draw-a-Horse simulation places focal persons in an experience in which, faced with a sudden need for leadership, they are expected to call on their natural, perhaps default, leadership behavior.

ACTIVITY 1.3

Draw-a-Horse

In this simulation, either an existing or newly formed team is assembled to perform a drawing task. The teams gather near a flipchart or whiteboard, but no markers are initially visible. Further, the members of the teams are not told by the coach or activity coordinator what they will be drawing, just that two instructions will be given prior to beginning the task.

Next, team roles are distributed. The principal role is the role of "leader" and is assigned to the individual who is the self-professed best drawer in the group. If, however, the activity has been organized by a coach for the benefit of a particular learner, then regardless of the learner's drawing ability, he or she should volunteer to be the designated leader for the exercise. The next role is that of the "observer," who does not participate in the drawing activity but rather observes the designated leader using the observer sheet in Figure 1.3, which is filled out during the activity. If the group is fairly large—say above six people in all—two observers can be selected to share the observation of the points highlighted on the sheet. The remaining members of the group are designated merely as "workers."

With the roles now assigned, the coach announces the start of the exercise by asking all the teams to pay heed to the final two instructions. At this time, the coach says—as instruction number one—that the teams will be drawing a horse. He or she then passes out one marker to each of the designated leaders. The teams are now set to hear the second instruction and thereafter to begin their drawing of a horse. At this time, the coach instructs each of the leaders to hand his or her marker to one of the workers. It is further directed that this same leader never touch the marker again, but that any and all workers may do so. The coach then just utters the words: "Please begin."

Faced with the need to complete an assignment but without the key tool to do so, the leaders and team are faced with the predicament of how to begin. All the leaders have at their disposal are their words. How will they proceed? Will they begin by offering immediate instructions or will they instinctively share control? What will be their primary mission as a leader? Will they display an interest in serving their team or will their primary objective be to obtain a superior product, no matter how it will be accomplished? These and other comparable behaviors are the precise points that the observers will evaluate using the observer sheet shown in Figure 1.3.

Meanwhile, the teams should be hard at working completing the task of drawing a horse. Some might be seen plunging ahead with a drawing; others might choose to develop a strategy beforehand, even to a consideration of what kind of horse to draw. The instructions did not specify that the horse be a conventional animal, for example. Some teams, perhaps through the encouragement of the leader, will involve each and every worker; in others only some of the workers may be drawing. The drawings will emerge with varying characteristics and frills; for example, some may have backgrounds. Teams may be encouraged to name their horses. Although there is no expressed time limit, once the coach sees that teams are beginning to finish up, he or she may announce that there is just, say, three minutes left. That way, teams will finish at approximately the same time.

Once the coach announces that time is up, and prior to any feedback from the observers, the horses may be evaluated, especially if there are more than two teams participating. There are countless ways to manage the evaluation process, so coaches can use their judgment. For example, participants in the room can evaluate all the other horses except their own. They could provide a

FIGURE **1.3**

Draw-a-Horse Observer Sheet

Instructions: Make notes as you observe the 'leader' interacting with the team members during the course of this activity, using the points listed below. It is important that you record specific examples of these points. After the exercise is over, be prepared to provide feedback to the leader in front of the team members. Ask the team to join in during this discussion to provide their own feedback to the leader, and, in particular, to give examples of their views. Be aware that your observations do not necessarily suggest better or worse leadership behavior. They are just a report of what you saw.

As you observe the leader in action, is he or she:

- Allowing the team members to share control of the task or is he or she taking control from the start?

- Displaying an interest in serving them or is he or she most interested in getting a superior product however it may be accomplished?

- Allowing decisions to be made by whoever has the best idea or ultimately making most of the decisions for the team, especially when there are differences?

- Encouraging everyone to speak freely and on behalf of the team or is he or she speaking most of the time?

- Encouraging team members to work through any problems on their own or assuring them that they can rely on him or her if they run into difficulty?

- Behaving as he or she would in a real-life predicament? (Feel free to save this point for the debriefing since you may not know how the leader normally behaves.)

quantitative score (say, assigning a number from 1 to 10) and/or they could be invited to provide qualitative comments directly on the drawing, using markers now freely distributed to all. Once scores and comments have been provided, perhaps using a gallery walk, teams should return to their own drawing to peruse the technical feedback. If qualitative commentaries have been produced, there are typically a number of humorous and off-handed remarks to take in. If quantitative scores have been provided, there will likely be a winner of the best drawing, for which the coach may wish to present an award.

After the merriment has subsided, the teams proceed to the main focus of the exercise—feedback to the leader as moderated by the observers now equipped with their filled-out observer sheets. Other team members should be encouraged to chime in to help the observers with relevant examples of the issues raised. The leader should also be informed that the observer sheet items are expressly designed to illustrate leaderful behaviors.

The teams should debrief the leader fully. Even though only one person has been chosen to be the focal learner for the exercise, other members will be vicariously assessing how they might have handled the simulation had they volunteered to assume the leader role. The coach can encourage this wider reflection after the leader has been fully debriefed. However, make sure that the debriefing is as specific as possible. How did the presumptive leader handle the assignment, especially at the outset? Teams may find it interesting to hear about an instance when one leader—who happened to have been a very good drawer—grabbed the palm of one of the workers and veritably traced a horse on the flipchart!

When the debriefing has run its course, the coach assembles all the teams for a plenary review of some of the leaderful principles brought into view. What leaderful behaviors are more or less natural to perform? What would it take to transition to more leaderful practices? Are such practices always advisable? If not, when are they more or less called for? Some of these reflections should also be committed to the learners' journals and subsequently brought up in dialogue with their own coaches and colleagues.

The Leaderful Mindset

Leaderful behavior does not view leadership in the familiar way of one person having direct influence over another. To the extent there is influence in the leadership relationship, it is mutual rather than one-way. Thus, all members of the community or entity are invited to advocate their positions on any matter, often on behalf of the greater common good of the enterprise, but at the same time they are equally sensitive to the views and feelings of others. In that sense, they are interested in a dialogue that can co-create their organization. Through dialogue, they commit to an engagement that takes the stance of nonjudgmental inquiry in which they express genuine curiosity about others and their views and in which they relax any initial preconceptions they have about such views. This form of collaborative dialogue often produces something new or unique from the inquiry that can reconstruct everyone's view of reality.

Conducting a collaborative dialogue of this nature is not always welcomed in our culture, which may prefer advancing one's point of view in such a way as to convince others of its inherent rightness. The one who is listened to is the one who can make his or her voice heard above the roar of the crowd. Such individuals do what they can to position themselves accordingly. The leaderful mindset tends toward greater humility in its belief that anything one accomplishes is usually dependent upon the contributions of others. The leaderful mindset may be natural to some individuals; it can also be developed through coaching that can bring out its latent properties.

The next activity, called "Squash," is designed to differentiate learners on the basis of their initial mindset regarding the requisite behavior to take advantage of a situation that could be characterized as power dependent.

....

ACTIVITY 1.4

Squash

This activity comes in the form of a short hypothetical scenario that requires the learner to make a decision about his or her prospective action when faced with an opportunity for personal and professional advancement. The specified action is thought to be an indication of mindset—the cognitive likelihood of action when faced with a situation that is power dependent. Will learners approach the scenario from an individualistically derived instrumental orientation, or will they react more collectively, deploying a moral orientation consistent with prospective leaderful practice?

After indicating their decision on the action they would take, they consider a number of questions for discussion in their learning team or with their coach, which in due course turns to a discussion of the mindset of the "leaderful" leader.

> The hypothetical scenario: You are a department manager in a large enterprise. There are four levels of management above you, the top level representing the corporate vice president, Tony Rivers. You are a nationally

ranked amateur squash player but have not made that known throughout the organization, except to your close friends. It has come to your attention that the VP, Tony, is an avid squash player, though a mediocre player at best. You need to decide, "Should I try to arrange a game with the VP; if so, what would be the circumstances?"

In debriefing this scenario with learners, a number of questions may be raised, but here is some context for the ensuing discussion. The situation described can be thought of as power dependent in that it presents an opportunity for someone to assume power or advantage because of some resource to be brought to bear. In this case, the resource is the employee's expertise in a non-work-related activity. Another way to view the scenario is that it presents the employee with an opportunity to gain influence even though he or she doesn't have any formal authority within the organization. Under these circumstances, there is an opportunity to gain influence or power by exchanging one's resources—or currencies—for those of someone who is higher in authority. Thus, the player exchanges his or her skill at squash for exposure to the top level of the organization.

However, exchange is not the only way to build relationships within the work environment. Rather than build relationships based on exchange, why not build them on the basis of trust and integrity? In such relationships, responsibility between the parties becomes prime. No party places his or her interests above those of others, especially among one's peers. Each party can be counted on to fulfill his or her responsibilities to the other without reservation. Thus, the parties seek to build their relationship by sustaining the confidence that each has in the other's integrity.

As the debriefing of this scenario begins, the learner focuses on the following questions, as appropriate:

1. If you have chosen to arrange a game with the VP, under what circumstances would you proceed? For example, would you attempt to convert the game into a lesson? Or would you just play, but perhaps play down to the VP's level? How would you arrange the game? How would Tony, the VP, react? How would your colleagues react, assuming they found out you were playing squash with the VP?

2. If you chose not to arrange a game, why not? Wouldn't you be losing a chance to gain an advantage career-wise within the company? Perhaps you see signs of danger in playing such a high-stakes game; if so, what might they be?

3. Whether or not you chose to play, are there any ethical considerations in this decision? Consider some of these:

   • Do the ends, in this case the opportunity for advancement, justify the means?

- What if everyone in the organization were to use such non-work-related means to advance?
- What if a peer of yours advanced through comparable means?
- Is it a concern that an exchange, such as this one based on an athletic currency, may not be available to others?
- Is it useful or even fair for workers to advance in a large bureaucracy through such means?
- Would you be willing to communicate openly about a practice of this nature with your coworkers? With your family members?

4. After reflecting on these considerations, what does your initial decision in this scenario suggest about your default disposition in regard to the meaning of leadership? Last, and after reflecting on some of the considerations raised here, would you now in retrospect make the same decision? If not, what might you do differently?

Leaderful Practice and Organizational Citizenship

For leaderful practice to take hold in a group or organization, team members need initially to exhibit an interest in serving the group or organization without regard to exclusive self-interest. By definition, collective leadership requires a commitment to work with others to accomplish goals for everyone's betterment, not only one's own.

Since altruism is not an automatic norm for any group, individuals must often initiate citizenship behavior as a first step in inspiring the practice of leaderful behavior. As a coach, you should be aware of the components of such organizational or group citizenship behaviors to determine whether learners are aware of them, have shown evidence of actually practicing them, and have an interest in promoting their use.

Learners might also be advised that working with their coach or with their peers on practicing citizenship behavior is recommended because these behaviors are not typically rewarded in any formal way in most organizations. They are discretionary and only evolve as others adopt them as part of the culture of the group.

Research on organizational citizenship behaviors (OCBs) has found that these behaviors can apply toward individuals in a group or to the group or organization as a whole. Activity 1.5 features a questionnaire that assesses the learner on his or her OCB as it relates to a group or team and thus will be referred to as "group citizenship behavior."

ACTIVITY 1.5

Group Citizenship Behavior

Learners are first asked to complete for themselves the group citizenship behavior questionnaire appearing as Figure 1.4. If they are currently in a group, they are encouraged to have the other group members fill out the questionnaire on their behalf. There are no gimmicks in this instrument; the higher the score on each of the items, the greater the prospective group citizenship behavior. Thus, a perfect score would be 75. Learners next compare their own scores with the scores received from their teammates. Then, using some of the questions below, they are invited to reflect on the results with their coach and, if possible, with their teammates, to determine if they have tendencies toward citizenship behavior that, in turn, tends to suggest a predisposition toward leaderful practice.

Questions for Reflection

1. In which of these items do you score relatively high?
2. How do your self-scores differ from your teammates' scores of you?
3. Do your teammates agree on the items?
4. If there is variance across your scores, what might explain these deviations?
5. Are there any patterns in these scores?
6. Do you believe these scores represent an appropriate level of citizenship behavior?
7. Would you prefer to exhibit more citizenship behavior; and if so, what would it take to increase your behavior along these lines?
8. Would you be willing to exhibit more citizenship behavior even if others on your team did not appear to you to be doing the same?
9. What would the group look like if positive citizenship behavior became a norm?
10. What does it say about someone's view of leadership if he or she believes that a group should exhibit relatively high citizenship behavior as a norm?

....

FIGURE **1.4**

Group Citizenship Behavior Questionnaire*

Fill out this questionnaire about yourself and then have your teammates complete it about you.

Not at All	A Little	A Moderate Amount	A Lot	All the Time
1	2	3	4	5

To what extent does this member:					
1. Help others who have been absent	1	2	3	4	5
2. Willingly give time to help others who need help	1	2	3	4	5
3. Go out of his or her way to make everyone feel welcome	1	2	3	4	5
4. Show genuine concern toward other members	1	2	3	4	5
5. Show pride when representing the group	1	2	3	4	5
6. Offer ideas to help improve the functioning of the group	1	2	3	4	5
7. Competently complete assigned tasks	1	2	3	4	5
8. Perform important tasks not expected of him or her	1	2	3	4	5
9. Take time to listen to other members	1	2	3	4	5
10. Attend all group meetings	1	2	3	4	5
11. Give advance notice when unable to make meetings	1	2	3	4	5
12. Help set positive group norms	1	2	3	4	5
13. Take initiative in moving the group forward	1	2	3	4	5
14. Help the group overcome obstacles	1	2	3	4	5
15. Come up with innovative ideas	1	2	3	4	5

* Adapted from scales in the domain of organizational citizenship behavior (OCB). In particular, see K. Lee and N. J. Allen, "Organizational Citizenship Behavior and Workplace Deviance: The Role of Affect and Cognitions," *Journal of Applied Psychology*, 87, pp. 131–142, 2002; and C. A. Smith, D. W. Organ, and J. P. Near, "Organizational Citizenship Behavior: Its Nature and Antecedents," *Journal of Applied Psychology*, 68, pp. 653–663, 1983.

....

Leaderful "Hang Time"

Even though many of us recognize that our learning and decision making can improve when we commit to reflect carefully on our decisions, we tend to move quickly. Although in many circumstances we have to act fast, there is great value in slowing down to reflect on our decision making so that we can obtain a greater appreciation for our assumptions in use. We can also learn more effectively when we slow down both during and after our experience so that we may draw new insights that allow us to reframe how we are approaching the decision in question. Oftentimes, our learning can be enhanced through the collective reflection of others who can lend further insight into our assumptions or about our emotional reactions attending to an event. In this way, we can learn to increase our "hang time," the figurative time in the air (as in a jump before making a play in the game of basketball) before we come back down to earth and proceed to our next step.

In the "Nine Shapes" exercise to follow, learners are invited to examine a critical challenge or incident confronting them from a variety of different perspectives, thus increasing their "hang time."

....

ACTIVITY 1.6

The Nine Shapes

To complete this activity, assemble a group of up to ten learners who might be willing to examine and help one of them in particular confront a critical challenge facing him or her at the moment.

1. Inform them that except for the one person with the problem—call him or her the *protagonist* (who could also be your principal client)—they will be examining a critical issue from multiple perspectives and that each will be given a "shape," representing a unique perspective. (See shapes on page 20.) Their assignment is to probe into the challenge the protagonist is about to disclose to them from the perspective of the shape described.

2. Hand out a different shape to each of the ten members, except, of course, for the protagonist. If there are fewer than ten people, one or more members can be asked to represent more than one perspective. Be sure to give members sufficient time to learn their shape sufficiently so that they can bring out the relevant perspective. During this time, it is preferable to have the protagonist leave the room.

Here are the nine shapes that the members will represent respectively in the ensuing conversation. Members may trade shapes if some would prefer one over another.

 Minus You tend to point out any omitted details or facts

 Plus You like to ask about the benefits of any plan for change and what difference it would make if it succeeds

 Stop Sign You point out the cautions, constraints, and contradictions and ask about the things that can prevent the plan from succeeding

 Yellow Sign You point out the ways that any cautions, constraints, and contradictions can be overcome

 Light Bulb You like to bring up new, even wild, ideas and alternatives

 Question Mark You like to ask about the assumptions underlying the approach being taken

 Connector You look for connections among disparate ideas and point out emerging patterns or principles

 Heart You like to ask about any gut feelings toward the plan

 Arrow You focus on next steps and ask if the planning can make way for implementation

3. Now have the protagonist describe the critical challenge that he or she is facing (could be in his or her personal life or professional practice) and how he or she plans to overcome it.

4. After a full explanation by the protagonist, turn the conversation over to the other members. They should discuss the protagonist's problem without necessarily involving him or her except in instances where there is a need to clarify the pressing challenge. Otherwise, the protagonist should focus not on any answers to questions raised, but on the questions themselves and comments made on the challenge from the varying perspectives. The protagonist takes notes on some of the new ways being suggested to look at the problem. Encourage the protagonist to note new insights that arise, even beyond the instant issue. He or she should feel free to ask questions of the questioners and commentators to probe any nuance from the point of view of their perspective.

5. After the conversation has been completed, ask the protagonist to make any comments he or she would like and then to explain to the team how he or she now views the challenge and any possible plan of response. For fun, you could ask the protagonist if he or she can identify which perspectives his or her colleagues were representing (though in this case the team members should have concealed their shape).

6. Now ask if everyone is prepared to debrief the activity. Talk through what was learned and how the use of the shapes might have changed normal operating discourse. What was it like for the protagonist to be more an observer of a discourse about his or her problem than an active participant? What new insights were drawn from looking at a problem from such diverse perspectives? Which perspectives were most insightful to the protagonist? How did the members of the group find the experience of representing a perspective, either familiar or not familiar to them? Is there a way to apply the "nine shapes" in regular work practice? Be sure that everyone takes some time to write in their journals for future dialogue with their own coaches.

CASE STUDY

Hang Time: Suspension above the Problem

VICTORIA MARSICK, JUDY O'NEIL, AND KAREN WATKINS

As part of our coaching work in action learning, in addition to supporting a team's learning as it works on a project, we also work with the individuals on the team in their leadership development. The exercise known as "Hang Time" was developed as a structured protocol for reflection within action learning programs and has many similarities to the "Leaderful Hang Time" section and the "Nine Shapes" exercise (Activity 1.6) in this fieldbook.

At the beginning of the exercise, we advise:

> It is both an art and practice to suspend yourself above the problem. The more hang time in the air . . . the better to see the "big" picture. The joy and the work is in the *ride*.

Framing the Problem

The following case describes the use of the "Hang Time" exercise in an action learning program designed for leadership development in a global pharmaceutical company. Bob, one of the participants in the program, asked for help with his communication skills.

In what follows, we initially describe Bob's responses to a set of reflective questions and activities suggested by his coach to help frame the problem. Next we describe a process composed of three steps—Q-Storming, Assumption Sharing, and Problem Reframing—that involves team members in a sharing experience very much in keeping with the Nine Shapes approach in which members ask questions or suggest avenues for attacking the problem. Many of Bob's initial responses were shared not just with his coach but also with his action-learning team members.

COACH: Can you share with me what your most pressing problem is in your role that you need to address right now? Please state the problem or challenge in the form of a question. [We have found that putting the challenge in the form of a question orients the client toward a reflective stance, which represents the first step in the practice of suspension.]

BOB: *How can I improve my listening skills and leadership in stressful situations?*

COACH: What is the background to this problem? What is the rationale for your current behavior?

BOB: *In stressful situations, I tend to drive decisions. I stop listening. I stop delegating. I see myself as the expert, the person who can best solve the problem. I've thought that by behaving this way, I can make life easier for my direct reports (DRs). I have this issue with customers and peers as well.*

COACH: Can you tell us who the key stakeholders are? What is your role?

BOB: *This is a new group in the company. We have no set processes. As the head of the department, I think I have to guide them more than perhaps I should.*

COACH: What are the barriers you must consider in coming to a solution? Consider, for example, such constraints as time, resources, scope, attitudes, power, personalities, and structure.

BOB: *Since I'm just getting to know my group, I'm not completely sure what to do. There isn't enough time to have group meetings to engage people. I don't feel entirely comfortable when direct reports show initiative because I'm not sure they're right in their approach.*

COACH: What solutions have you already tried and how did they turn out?

BOB: *I've tried casual hallway conversations, but things haven't improved sufficiently. I've held "status" meetings but not meetings to just hear them out or to let them influence me so I can begin to see they have ideas.*

Working with Bob

The next phase of our version of "Hang Time" corresponds to the "Nine Shapes" approach, except that team members do not act out of a role or orientation. Using what we call Q-Storming, Assumption Sharing, and Problem Reframing, they derive their own genuine inquiries about, in this case, Bob's problem. In Q-Storming, team members first write down questions of a clarifying nature, followed by questions of a reflective or interpretive nature. They share their questions in a round-robin format, one question at a time. The problem holder does not talk while listening to the questions but may share a few insights at the end of the step.

In the course of Q-Storming, some of the questions that were posed of Bob included:

- How do you know your people think their life is easier when you act as the expert?
- What would it take to make you trust people?
- Who else at work is this a problem for?
- How can you find out what your people really know?
- Who back at work could help you with this?
- What's the worst thing that will happen if you don't improve?

After reflecting on these and other questions, Bob expressed the following initial insight: "I hadn't really thought about the issue from a trust perspective. I've been thinking about it as an issue with my expertise."

In the Assumption Sharing step of the exercise, team members share their assumptions using the same format as the Q-Storming step. Their assumptions are often of this sort: "I think I'm right when I say . . ." or "If I were you, I would assume . . ." The assumptions presented to Bob included:

- People who work for you recognize when you're operating in this mode and just get out of your way. There's probably even an early warning system.
- Some of your people know almost as much as you do.
- You're willing to put up with the stress because you want to be the problem solver.
- You need to more clearly define the role of what it means to be a leader to understand how to change this behavior.
- You'll need to let go of the need to be right.

Upon further reflection on some of these challenging assumptions, Bob remarked, "I do need to make some choices about what's important for me as a leader—what do I owe my people, the company, myself."

During the Problem Reframing portion of the exercise, team members suggest how they would reframe the question given the new data revealed in the prior steps. In this instance, they provided some feedback to Bob on what they thought his problem really was about—their reframes of his initial question:

- How can I learn enough about my people that I can trust them with important decisions?
- How do I learn when it's more important to develop my people than to always be right?

Conclusion and Debrief

We ask the problem holder how difficult it was "hanging" in the problem-defining mode rather than trying to solve the problem immediately. Both coaches and peer mentors inquire how the problem holder might view the problem differently after going through the experience.

After the "Hang Time" exercise, Bob returned to his job and began to work on his problem equipped with the new insights. Later in the program, he shared the following with the team:

> "I consciously schedule time with my DRs to talk about important decisions. I open myself up to listen rather than jump in with solutions. It still feels strange, but I hope it will eventually feel natural. I've asked the team to have meetings themselves. I also assign them projects to solve and I take their recommendations. It seems to work very well. I'm feeling more comfortable in letting go."

In this case, the "Hang Time" exercise helped to create a greater and deeper understanding of how leadership can be viewed in an organization. Bob learned that being the expert wasn't as important as helping his people grow in knowledge and confidence. The exercise is able to generate this kind of leaderful change by helping make what may be a tacit understanding more explicit, identifying the "real" problem, and asking the participant to share some of his or her deepest motives and values behind any actions taken.

Chapter Two

Interpersonal-Level Change

WHILE A COACH CAN HELP AN INDIVIDUAL DISCOVER his or her inner self, ultimately any person's identity is shaped by others; in other words, our self is formed as much by others' perceptions of us as by what we do. Thus, interpersonal dialogue is important as a way to discover wisdom about oneself through others' eyes as well as through our own. Coaches can assist participants in learning teams not so much to mount arguments to win a debate, but rather to encourage them to share their reflections and solicit those of others. Reflective learners become sensitive to why things are done in a certain way. They inquire about the values that are manifested behind any behavior. They learn to uncover discrepancies between what is being said and what is being done. They show an interest in probing into the forces below the surface that may be shaping actions and outcomes.

Through engagement in dialogue, participants learn not only to present their own viewpoints but to inquire about the views of others. In this way, they attempt to balance advocacy with inquiry. Inquiry, though, does not have to take the form of an interrogation, which frequently appears in the form of a blistering set of questions. Although questions might be very effective, they should be supplemented by patient active listening that encourages the speaker to say as much as he or she wishes to say on the subject.

Questioning can also be supplemented by surfacing our own attributions or inferences. An *attribution* is merely a perception that assigns a cause to a particular event. An *inference* is the process of arriving at a conclusion often based on false premises. As human beings, we cannot help forming attributions and inferences about others. Yet these perceptions are unfortunately inaccurate at times. If people act on them, and the assumptions and inferences are inaccurate, the subsequent actions can lead to unintended consequences.

In promoting dialogue, a coach can help learners surface these assumptions. Once the learner has brought them into view, he or she can ask others to verify their accuracy. So, once we agree on our common and different meanings, we can begin to reconstruct our projects together on a more solid footing.

The field of action science refers to the rethinking process that helps us discover our often hidden meanings as "reflection-in-action" or contemporaneous reflection. In order to engage in reflection-in-action, learners start by offering a frame of the situation at hand. Then, if in a group situation, they can inquire as to how others see it. They thereupon reflect upon these frames and subsequently begin to surface and test their underlying assumptions and reasoning processes. The ultimate aim is to narrow inconsistencies between our espoused theories and theories-in-use. *Espoused theories* are those characterizing what we say we will do. *Theories-in-use* describe how we actually behave, although their revision of our espoused values is often tacit. The goal of interpersonal coaching is to uncover these theories-in-use, in particular to distinguish between those that inhibit and those that promote learning.

To assist learners in undertaking systemic change, interpersonal coaches often create real-time experiments (perhaps using the client's colleagues as role players) to help learners focus on their mental models—those representations that explain our thought processes about how we see things working in the real world. For example, coaches might elicit the attributions and evaluations learners are making about themselves, about others, or about the system under scrutiny. Or they might ask learners to slow down and reflect upon the inferential steps taken in leaping from data to conclusions.

The seven activities in this chapter are designed to help coaches work with learners to engage in more meaningful interpersonal interactions.

The first activity, **Practicing Dialogic Skills**, helps learners acquire and then practice a set of advanced dialogic skills to help them engage in deeper and more productive interpersonal conversations.

The second activity, **Left-Hand Column**, is designed to help learners surface some of the unfortunate assumptions and inferences they make during difficult conversations, first in private and safe consultation with colleagues and ultimately during real conversations with others in a way that might lead to more effective mutual action.

The third activity, **Balancing Advocacy with Inquiry**, gives learners an opportunity to try out a practice conversation in which inquiry is purposely emphasized, leading prospectively to greater balance with the act of advocacy.

The fourth activity, **The "Stolen" Idea Case**, allows learners to review a range of engagement styles, especially when faced with a potential conflict arising from an interaction with a colleague. The collaborating style is proposed to result in greater deployment of leaderful behavior compared to alternative styles.

The fifth activity, **Practicing What I Preach**, engages learners in a simulation with colleagues who role-play team members whom they plan to approach regarding an intervention that is designed to change the team to become more democratic in its practices.

The sixth activity, **Journeys to Engage Our Intercultural Competence**, presents learners with the opportunity to develop their intercultural sensitivity as part of their emerging portfolio of interpersonal skills, through the undertaking of a cross-cultural journey to discover more about the self through others.

The seventh activity, **Peer Coaching Using Action Learning**, is designed to lighten the burden of the coach by involving the learner's peers in coaching each other when faced with a pressing business or organizational challenge.

Dialogic Skills

Activity 2.1 is a lengthy one that introduces the five advanced skills of reflective practice—being, speaking, disclosing, testing, and probing—displayed in Figure 2.1. Although the skills may be difficult to master, the interpersonally competent individual can learn each of these skills, observe them in an interpersonal situation, and deploy them when called for. It is not necessary for all the parties to a dialogue to practice these skills at the same time; rather, it is merely important that the skills be available in one's toolkit to help overcome obstacles or to enrich the dialogue.

In Figure 2.1, initially designed by my colleague, Robert Leaver, and myself, the two dimensions (staying with self and inquiring with others) are listed across the top of the figure, and the three modes of dialogue

FIGURE **2.1**

Five Advanced Dialogic Skills

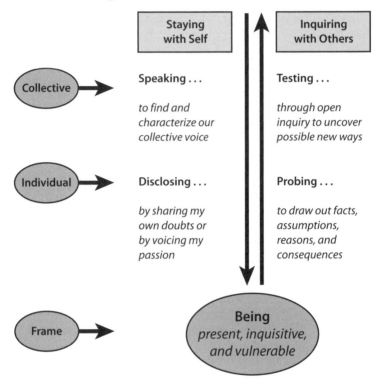

(collective, individual, frame) are depicted on the left side. In terms of the modes, the "frame" mode refers to how you think about a situation, or, more specifically, how you select, name, and organize facts to create a story about what is going on and what to do in a particular situation. In the individual mode, you hear your own voice or address one individual at a time, whereas in the collective mode, you extend your contributions and inquiry to all the members in the interpersonal setting. In terms of the cross dimensions, at times, you make personal contributions to the group or focus attention on yourself. At other times, you extend and dedicate attention to others.

As preparation for this exercise, it is advisable to engage learners in a tutorial to understand the five advanced dialogic skills. On the page that follows, the five skills are defined along with a listing of their behavioral manifestations, followed by a self-inquiry to help bring out the skill in question. An example of each skill is provided. Since there are five skills, it is ideal to undertake this exercise with five people, though more or less than five would be manageable. If there are more than five, some of the skills can be doubled up; if there are fewer than five, some of the skills would be divided up. Learners should review all the skills, but ultimately each will be assigned one of the five to focus on.

SKILL DESCRIPTIONS

Being

Definition:	Creates a climate for reflection. It asks that we experience or describe situations, even our own involvement in them, without imputing meaning
Behavior:	View with empathy and with open-hearted acceptance, as if you are a close friend or family member
	View as strange—to display deep interest and curiosity
	Invite questions and comments
	Acknowledge one's own and others' vulnerability
	Consider positions as hypotheses to be tested
	Pause—Reflect—Contemplate
Self-Inquiry:	What can I learn here?
	How am I acting to constrain what is possible?
Example:	"It looks like we have pretty much endorsed the direct marketing approach for this advertising campaign. As you know, I have pushed for it as well, but we all remember what happened on the Do-op project. I have to admit that direct marketing feels right to me, but to be honest with you, I still have some reservations. Do you think we should take one more look at this? I'm afraid I might have overlooked something."

Speaking

Definition:	Calls for speaking with a collective voice to find collective meaning; attempts to characterize the state of a group of colleagues at a given time

Behavior:	Suggest group norms
	Articulate meaning, such as by summoning an image
	Be willing to bring out uncertainties and unfounded assumptions
Self-Inquiry:	What can I say to help us understand ourselves?
	What social practices are we engaging in right now?
	What is emerging in our collective consciousness that I can articulate?
Example:	"Jamie, your concern left me with an image that seems to characterize our effort right now. It is like we're a cargo plane having to make our destination to Istanbul but with one engine knocked out."

Disclosing

Definition:	Asks that members find and speak with their own voice in order to disclose their doubts and assumptions as well as voice their impatience and passion
Behavior:	Disclose one's feelings at a given moment, based on what has transpired
	Present one's story to reveal the depth of one's experience
Self-Inquiry:	What am I holding back that needs to be aired?
	What might I say to help others know me better?
Example:	"I wasn't planning on telling you about this. I know I have seemed distracted lately and the way I just dealt with Linda is a case in point. Well, frankly, I am having some marital problems. I've moved into an apartment and can't get my mind off my kids."

Testing

Definition:	Makes an open-ended query to others to attempt to uncover new ways of thinking and behaving; asks members of a group to consider their own process, including their norms, roles, and past actions

Behavior:	Make a "meta-inquiry" to focus on where the group is right now
	Ask whether the group would be willing to test some taken-for-granted assumptions
Self-Inquiry:	Are we helping each other right now?
	What can I ask to help us all focus on our process right now?
Example:	"I guess we're at an impasse. In fact, it looks like we're split right down the middle on this one. Can we come up with some way to resolve this to everyone's reasonable satisfaction? What do you all think?"

Probing

Definition:	Inquires directly with others to understand the facts, reasons, assumptions, inferences, and possible consequences of a given suggestion or action; commits to a nonjudgmental consideration of another's views
Behavior:	Ask about another's impressions and perceptions
	Inquire about one's attributions of another's behavior
	Explore the consequences of an alternative
Self-Inquiry:	What is the basis for another person's point of view and feelings?
	Can I explore with others even though their position may be different from my own?
Example:	"Frank, you've said several times that you believe that the workers in your unit should take the ball and run with it. Yet you say they are dependent and continue to check with you on every new initiative. Is there anything you might be doing or saying that might be blocking their sense of independence? Might you be unwittingly giving them the sense that you'll be critical if they screw up, for example?"

Having completed the tutorial, learners are now ready to complete the activity.

ACTIVITY 2.1

Practicing Dialogic Skills

STEP 1: Start by having learners engage in a dialogue with their colleagues. If they are part of a team, it is ideal to proceed with a normal team meeting that is already scheduled, as long as the session contains time for a free-ranging discussion of a critical issue affecting the team. Continue the discussion for about 15 minutes.

STEP 2: Stop the discussion and ask each team member to assume one of the five dialogic skills. Learners can choose a skill based on their current or prospective ability. For example, perhaps someone would like to try out a skill heretofore untapped. Each team member spends some additional private time learning to execute the acquired skill.

STEP 3: Resume the discussion with each of the learners holding to his or her role. To ensure discussion flow, they don't need to practice their skill at each utterance, but they must do so, say, once during each 3- to 5-minute span of time.

STEP 4: In your role as coach, you may want to observe the proceedings, making notes using the observer sheet depicted as Figure 2.2. If you would prefer not to be the observer, ask one of the learners if he or she might assume the role of observer for the duration of the team discussion during which members are practicing their respective dialogic skills. It would be most helpful if the observer is personally knowledgeable about both the participants and about the team as a whole. Try not to notice which skills were chosen by the participants. After enough time has transpired to collect sufficient data, time is called and the observers begin a debriefing session with the team.

FIGURE **2.2**

Observer Sheet

1. Follow the discussion as carefully as you can and note any changes in the behavior of particular colleagues or team members. What specific statements or queries are individuals using that are helpful? Not helpful?

2. Try to determine how this discussion might be different from the usual interpersonal interactions involving these colleagues. If you know these people, did they interact differently than usual? Note any differences.

3. Would you say that this team meeting was more or less effective than typical team discussions? Note any differences.

4. Were members of the team able to stay in their assigned dialogic roles, or did they lapse out of them? What was difficult about staying in role?

5. Finally, which of these dialogic skills will the team wish to retain? How will the team remember to use them?

Broadening Our Dialogue

An approach called "Left-Hand Column," which is based on the work of Chris Argyris and the principals of the firm Action Design, has been developed to help people broaden their dialogue with one another. It holds to the view that in couching or overcontrolling our language in our discourse with one another, we may limit the opportunity to learn from each other and even to make effective decisions together. So, trying to be diplomatic to avoid upsetting people can actually have a reverse effect of not achieving our mutual objectives.

··

ACTIVITY 2.2

Left-Hand Column

This activity can be used to debrief an encounter that did not go well, or it can be used to prepare for an anticipated difficult conversation. The result in either case should be greater understanding on the part of learners about how to merge some of their private conversation with their public conversation in a way that would be productive for the parties. It can help them reinterpret some of the immediate conclusions drawn from their on-the-spot reasoning, which, in turn, could lead to a revised approach to dialogue. Further, with more data on the table, there is less need for them or their colleagues to "one-up" each other, resulting in more leaderful behavior as they mutually plan endeavors or prepare to work together.

To begin, you can work with one or more of the learners by asking them to think of a recent conversation that did not go well and did not move one of their key projects or activities forward. Make sure it is a relationship (such as with a peer or a boss) that they consider to be important to them. As noted previously, learners could also think of an impending conversation for planning purposes.

As they think of the conversation, ask them to consider these four questions:

1. What did the other person(s) say or do that you found upsetting (evoked a negative emotional response in you)?
2. What did you say or do in response (all you need is this one exchange)?
3. What were you thinking and feeling that you chose not to say?
4. What negative result came out of this conversation?

The way that they prepare their answers to these questions characterizes this activity as the "left-hand column." Learners prepare their answers on a sheet that looks like Figure 2.3. First, they draw a line down the middle of the page. On the right side, they indicate, using a transcript format, what they and their boss (or colleague) said and did. On the left side, they write out those thoughts and feelings that they chose not to say. They finish by indicating on the bottom of the right side what the consequences of the conversation were that concern them now.

After they have prepared their transcript, learners work with you or with a close colleague to debrief this activity. They should be prepared to work through the following steps:

STEP 1: They explain to you the details of both columns so that you understand the dynamics of the situation.

FIGURE **2.3**

The Left-Hand Column Transcript

My Thoughts and Feelings	What We Said and Did
What I was thinking and feeling that I chose not to say	Them: (what they said or did that upset you)
	Me: (what you said or did in response)
	Them:
	Me:
	[List any additional exchanges]
	Result: (the consequences that concern you)

STEP 2: They clarify what they were hoping to achieve in the exchange with their boss or colleagues and what made them unhappy about the results.

STEP 3: As a coach, pursue the following points with them:

a. How did you interpret what the other person said or did? In retrospect, are there alternative interpretations to consider?

b. If you had interpreted your boss's or colleague's actions or statements in some of these alternative ways, would you have drawn different conclusions? What implications would this have had on the actions that were taken?

STEP 4: Review with the learners whether there are parts of their left-hand column that they might have been able to bring out, given some of the new reasoning. How might they have restated some of these into nondefensive inquiries or even puzzles?

STEP 5: Last, discuss with them what they might have learned from going through this activity.

Increasing Our Inquiry

It is often the case that we can improve the quality of our interpersonal interactions by following a recommendation of one of my colleagues, Bill Torbert: increase our inquiry in relation to our advocacy. *Advocacy*, which tends to dominate in most conversations, occurs when we put forward our points of view on any subject. It provides new information and in its deeper form can illuminate our reasoning and even personal feelings about a topic. Most of us tend to advocate quite well; however, if we do so at the exclusion of inquiry, our points of view may come across as imposing rather than as proposing.

It is *inquiry*, however, that can truly enrich a conversation because it extends unadulterated attention to the speaker or speakers. Inquiry comes in two forms: it asks speakers how and why they view the subject in the way advanced, and it asks others what they think about what you just said. In both cases, as long as it is a legitimate request for information and not an advocacy or an intimidation disguised as a question (for example, "Are you sure that your method is superior to Peter's?"), inquiry in combination with sound advocacy can lead to mutual learning between the parties. Mutual learning, in turn, suggests a humility underlying leaderful practices in which any one person acknowledges that his or her contributions are dependent upon the contributions of others.

The artful combination of advocacy and inquiry is depicted in Figure 2.4 on the next page and, like the prior activity, is based on the work of Chris Argyris and the firm Action Design.

FIGURE **2.4**

Balancing Advocacy and Inquiry*

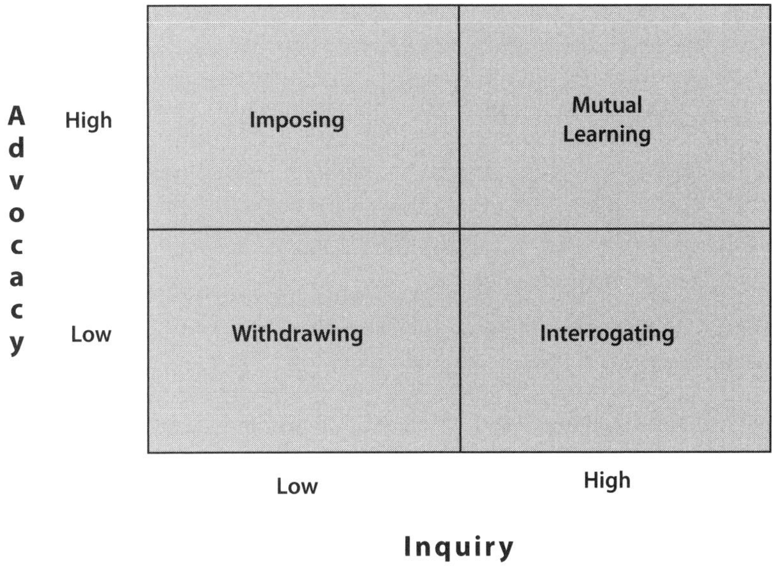

*Copyright © Action Design. Used by permission.

ACTIVITY 2.3

Balancing Advocacy with Inquiry

In this concise activity, learners converse with a group of accepting colleagues who might be meeting about a topic of interest. The group first needs to be apprised of the value of balancing advocacy with inquiry as per the preceding tutorial. They should be informed that in your role as coach, you will be amending the conversation with somewhat different rules from the norms of conventional conversation and that they'll all have a chance to debrief this format at the conclusion of the activity. The activity is loosely based on an approach used by Stephen Brookfield of St. Thomas University, called "Circle of Voices," and by Michael Marquardt in his action learning approach described in his book *Leading with Questions*.[8]

STEP 1: Have the group agree on a topic of interest that they would like to explore while learning about the value of balancing advocacy with inquiry.

STEP 2: Group members go around a circle and each member of the group offers his or her point of view on the topic. Do not hold to any regimented order; people offer their comments only when they are ready. However, no one else can interrupt by speaking or asking questions during this step. This step is considered completed only when every person has spoken.

STEP 3: During a period of reflection, each person writes down questions that they would like to ask to follow up on some of the comments offered by others in the group.

STEP 4: Group members have a full discussion about the topic, but in this step, participants in any order proceed to ask questions of one another. They cannot talk about their own ideas unless asked by someone else. Although somewhat unusual, the tenor of this conversation should focus on good questioning since it mobilizes the discussion. Without it, the conversation cannot proceed.

STEP 5: After 30–45 minutes, stop the conversation and ask whether there was, first of all, greater balance between advocacy and inquiry in the just-completed discussion. Do people believe that useful insight was achieved on the topic using this format? Is there any part of this approach that participants believe could be incorporated into their everyday conversation?

Engaging in Collaborative Behavior

It is often thought that when two or more parties get together to accomplish some task or set of tasks, there is little substitute for their cooperating to achieve the maximal advantage to each. However, one or more of the parties may believe that their solution to the problem at hand is clearly the best or that there is no other choice than to have things go their way. This approach is known as *assertive behavior*, in contrast to a *cooperating* style

---

[8] M. J. Marquardt, *Leading with Questions: How Leaders Find the Right Solutions by Knowing What to Ask* (San Francisco: Jossey-Bass, 2005).

in which one sees the need to please the other party as preferable to "winning at all costs."

When we combine these two overarching dimensions of cooperating and asserting, five styles of engagement, originally proposed as conflict-handling modes by Kenneth Thomas, can be formulated, and are listed and defined in Table 2.1.

In Figure 2.5, the five conflict-handling styles are mapped based on the two overarching dimensions of cooperation and assertiveness. Notice that collaborative behavior is depicted along the furthest point of the diagonal, constituting the maximum amount of *both* cooperation and assertiveness.

The literature in the domain of conflict management suggests that all five styles can be used favorably in particular circumstances. However,

TABLE **2.1**

The Five Conflict-Handling Styles*

1. *Avoiding* represents a withdrawal such that neither one's own nor the other party's concerns are satisfied. A typical response might be, "I'll think about it tomorrow."

2. *Accommodating* occurs when individuals or groups demonstrate a will to cooperate in satisfying others' concerns while at the same time acting unassertively in addressing their own needs. A typical response might be, "It will be my pleasure."

3. *Compromising* represents an intermediate behavior on both the assertiveness and cooperative dimensions. It calls for the sharing of positions to achieve an agreement that satisfies some of one's wants. A typical response might be, "Let's make a deal."

4. *Competing* occurs when individuals or groups try to satisfy their own concerns while demonstrating little willingness to satisfy the concerns of others. A typical response might be, "It's my way or the highway."

5. *Collaborating* emphasizes maximum satisfaction for both parties such that each exerts both assertive and cooperative behavior. Both parties encourage the mutual expression of their needs and concerns. A typical response might be, "We can work it out."

*Adapted from Kenneth W. Thomas, "Toward Multi-Dimensional Values in Teaching: The Example of Conflict Behaviors," *Academy of Management Review*, Vol. 2, No. 3, pp. 484–490, 1977. Used by permission of Kenneth W. Thomas.

FIGURE **2.5**

Conflict-Handling Styles Based on Degree of Cooperation and Assertiveness*

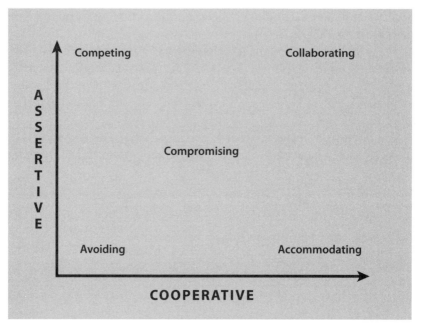

*Adapted from Kenneth W. Thomas, "Conflict and Conflict Management" in Marvin D. Dunnette, ed., *The Handbook of Industrial and Organizational Psychology* (Chicago: Rand McNally, 1976). Used by permission of Kenneth W. Thomas.

collaborating is considered the most apt method to enact leaderful practices. Collaborating is also called for under a number of conditions:

- When a solution needs to be maximized since the concerns of the parties are too important to resort to a compromise
- When the objective is to learn
- When insights from many sources and perspectives need to be merged
- When commitment is required of all the involved parties
- When the parties need to work through any feelings that have interfered with their ongoing relationship

Although collaboration typically takes more time than the other engagement strategies, since each party seeks to maximize his or her needs, it can lead to innovative solutions that may produce positive value to the parties. Indeed, it is thought to generate richer solutions among stakeholders to a problem than can be produced by any single participant. Further, collaboration tends to humanize the parties rather than depict them as opponents with the attending stereotypes. It leads to empathy and goodwill, which can lay the groundwork for an ongoing productive relationship.

ACTIVITY 2.4

The "Stolen" Idea Case

This activity presents a case that depicts a situation that could be handled by a variety of engagement styles, including collaborating. If possible, organize the activity by assembling a large enough group to divide up into subgroups, each representing one of the five engagement types referred to earlier.

STEP 1: Each subgroup first works on the advantages and disadvantages of its engagement style: avoiding, accommodating, compromising, competing, collaborating.

STEP 2: Each subgroup reads the case called "Stolen" Idea. They then, working out of their style, describe how they would deal with the colleague in the case and, if relevant, with the manager.

The "Stolen" Idea Case

Two supervisors have been working in separate operations units. As one of these supervisors, you have seven years seniority in the company while your colleague has two. One day while having lunch, you mention your idea to help increase productivity at no additional cost to the company. Your colleague asks questions about this idea.

Two weeks later at the monthly department meeting, the manager proudly announces that the company will be adopting the plan to be presented by one of the supervisors and asks that supervisor to present his ideas. It turns out to be your "friend," who proceeds to describe in detail the plan you presented to him over lunch.

You are disturbed that your colleague, whom you trusted, "stole" and claimed full credit for your idea.

STEP 3: After sufficient time to prepare the first two steps, each subgroup presents the advantages and disadvantages of its style without regard to the case, and then reacts to the case from the point of view of its respective style. How would the members—as an avoider or as a competer and so on—handle their colleague? Would they involve the manager; if so, in what way? Each subgroup responds to questions from others who are not familiar with the style being represented.

STEP 4: Debrief this activity by considering the often liberal differences in handling the players in the case from the perspective of the different styles. Pay attention to how the colleague is viewed from these different perspectives. Indeed, is it always clear that the idea was "stolen"? Might the accommodators or collaborators suggest that ideas in a group do not have to be "owned" by anyone and can be part of an emerging knowledge development process? If a team ultimately wishes to participate together as a leaderful entity, which style is most consistent with the leaderful tradition? Since collaboration is indeed one of the Four Cs of leaderful practice (along with concurrent, collective, and compassionate leadership), pay special attention to the collaborating style. Can collaborators work with all the other styles? How might they overcome any time pressure because collaboration is known to require more time than most of the other styles? Note that the acquisition of collaborating behavior may require an incorporation of some of the other skills depicted in this chapter on interpersonal-level change.

Consistency Between Espousal and Action

Public reflection can enhance our interpersonal relations on a number of fronts. By *public reflection*, we refer to the process of reflecting together with colleagues to surface the social, political, and emotional data from direct experience with others. These data can often become precisely those that might be blocking our operating effectiveness. For example, at times we may be unaware of the consequences of our behavior or that we are using data superficially. Perhaps most critical is our inconsistency between what we say we do or will do and what we actually do. Especially when it comes to such democratic values as being open and receptive to others, participating with them, listening deeply, or accepting others' emotions, we tend to deceive ourselves that we practice what we preach.

In Activity 2.5, learners commit to reducing the common inconsistency between their espousal and action by reducing their independent control over the situations they encounter, which contain a degree of stress or even of embarrassment, in favor of more mutual control. They learn to espouse their beliefs in a straightforward manner but at the same time make themselves open to the inquiry of others, even to the point of expressing their own vulnerability. In this way, they take advantage of all that others have to offer in surmounting any mutual challenges.

....

ACTIVITY 2.5

Practicing What I Preach

This activity is designed to help learners narrow the familiar inconsistency that most of us have between our espoused values and our actions, especially when our values are of a democratic nature, such as when we invite others to express themselves openly to us, to challenge us, and to participate with us. To get started, three to four colleagues are asked to join a key learner, whom we'll call a "protagonist," in a simulation of a prospective intervention that he or she would like to make in an actual team in which the protagonist is currently a member. The protagonist is thinking about an intervention that she or he would like to make with this team that would open it up more so that the team might face its problems more squarely. In other words, the protagonist would like to have this team become more democratic in its practices—more accepting of ideas from all its members or perhaps more participative in involving everyone, or even more caring.

STEP 1: The protagonist describes to the colleagues the team in which she or he is proposing to make an intervention (without detailing the intervention yet) and then characterizes in detail the other members of the team. The protagonist needs to be precise in these descriptions because each of his or her colleagues in this activity has to be prepared to role-play these other members of the team. Thus, they need to be equipped with as much information as possible about these other members, because during the subsequent simulation they will be asked to role-play the other members as if they were them. The only exception is that if you as coach prefer not to occupy the observer role, one of the protagonist's colleagues needs to be asked to be an observer who will be equipped with the observer sheet depicted in Figure 2.6 (page 47).

STEP 2: After characterizing the members of the team for which the protagonist is planning the intervention, the protagonist should temporarily depart to let the colleagues internalize the information shared with them so that they can prepare to role-play the simulation. All they need to know is that the protagonist will soon be approaching them with an intervention. At this point, the protagonist should first spend a few moments going over in his or her mind how he or she would like to approach the prospective intervention. Then, he or she should meet privately with the observer. In this meeting, he or she should describe to the observer the plans for the intervention. The protagonist should also disclose any democratic values that lie underneath the planned intervention: What is it that he or she is proposing that might lead to more democratic practices in this team?

STEP 3: The protagonist then returns with the observer to the team. Assuming the other colleagues are ready, begin the discussion of the intervention. The protagonists' colleagues, of course, respond in their roles. The protagonist, meanwhile, engages these colleagues—now in role—in the proposed intervention. Enough time is given to allow the parties to try to reach an agreement. The discussion ends when they have either reached an agreement or an impasse.

STEP 4: The debriefing of the activity is conducted by the observer, who will comment on the simulation using his or her notes. Naturally, the main purpose of the activity is to see whether or not the protagonist practiced what he or she preached when it comes to democratic values. In addition, the simulation tends to pick up on one's ability to inquire with others and to balance that inquiry against one's advocacy (as in Activity 2.3). After a full debriefing, the protagonist might discuss how he or she may have changed how he or she plans to approach the actual forthcoming intervention. You may suggest to the protagonist that he or she might also benefit from reconvening the group *after* the intervention to brief everyone on how things went and whether and to what extent he or she acquired the ability to narrow the gap between espousal and action.

Intercultural Competence

Coaching in the domain of interpersonal relationships often entails working with others to heighten their sensitivity to other cultures or subcultures. People in social groups develop their own ways of looking at the world and of learning how to behave in interaction with others. Yet, though an individual may relate well within her or his own culture, she or he may not have developed an intercultural competence when communicating within another culture. This requires the ability to initiate and respond to

FIGURE **2.6**

Observer Sheet for "Practicing What I Preach"

1. In the private debriefing with you, did your colleague (call him or her the protagonist) espouse any values behind his or her intentions for the forthcoming conversation? What were they, and were any of a democratic nature?

2. During the simulation, take notes as you observe whether or not the protagonist is actually practicing these espoused values voiced in question number 1:

    a. Give examples of how he or she is holding to these values.

    b. Give examples of where he or she is veering from these values.

3. Is the protagonist balancing inquiry with advocacy?

4. Is the protagonist practicing public reflection by questioning some of the assumptions underlying the problem at hand (for example, by getting the group to wonder together why the problem has been allowed to hang around)? How is she or he phrasing things to bring out these assumptions?

    a. What are some of the specific questions he or she is asking, and what is unfolding from this form of inquiry?

    b. If he or she is not asking such questions, what might one look like?

messages as if from within the new culture. Intercultural competence is thought to contain three dimensions: a *content* dimension that constitutes one's knowledge of another culture, an *affective* dimension that displays sensitivity to the members of the new culture, and a *behavioral* dimension that incorporates the skills necessary to manage intercultural situations.

In communicating with other cultures, we learn to overcome our false assumptions and stereotypes so as to develop a richer understanding of ourselves and others and to enhance our cultural sensitivity. We develop a keener appreciation of the perspectives of others, and when we understand them better, we can approach them more confidently as we embark on mutual projects.

....

ACTIVITY 2.6

Journeys to Engage Our Intercultural Competence

The purpose of this activity is to obtain direct experience to assess one's intercultural competence by taking a "journey" or a visit—of a reasonable depth—to a culture different from one's own. The journey could be to a subculture within one's own culture (for example, a visit to an urban community—such as to a soup kitchen—from a wealthy suburban neighborhood) or to an international location. There is evidence from intercultural research that journeys of even short durations can affect one's intercultural sensitivity, especially if the journey offers an opportunity for active and interactive involvement rather than mere passive observation.

Learning from activities of this nature—not unlike most described in this fieldbook—can be enhanced if the learner commits to a reflective process through the use of a journal or portfolio. These devices ask learners to self-select observations, experiences, and artifacts for representation. Entries should help the learner participate in and interpret cultural interactions.

STEP 1: In your role as coach, assist learners to develop a baseline of their current intercultural competence by assessing where they stand on several dimensions that characterize the handling of cultural differences. Learners initially draw a point where they believe they stand along the continuum of cultural adaptation (displayed in Figure 2.7) based on Bennett's six-stage development model of intercultural sensitivity and Hammer and Bennett's Intercultural Development Inventory.

FIGURE **2.7**

A Continuum of Cultural Adaptation*

Instructions: Place a star (★) where you believe you stand on this continuum. In the space below the continuum or in your journal, please write a justification for your choice.

Theme	Sample Justification
— Simplicity	There is little point in exploring differences; rather, we should just learn to get along and not try to change each other.
— Evaluation	People just have to accept that there are cultural differences and in some cases our culture is superior, and in other cases, theirs is.
— Similarity	At the heart of the matter, all of us humans are more or less the same with a few minor differences.
— Acceptance	There are some patterns suggesting some fairly significant and interesting differences to learn about between our culture and theirs.
— Accommodation	Given the important differences between our culture and theirs, I would seek to alter my perceptions and behavior to accommodate their culture.
— Integration	I would seek to incorporate another culture's idiosyncrasies into my own so as to achieve a multicultural identity.

The reason that I placed the star where I did:

*Adapted from the Developmental Model of Intercultural Sensitivity in M. J. Bennett, "Toward Ethnorelativism: A Developmental Model of Intercultural Sensitivity," pp. 27–71 in R. M. Paige, ed., *Education for Intercultural Experience*. (Yarmouth, ME: Intercultural Press, 1993); and from the Intercultural Development Inventory, see: M. R. Hammer, and M. J. Bennett. *The Intercultural Development Inventory (IDI) Manual* (Portland, OR: Intercultural Communication Institute, 1998).

STEP 2: Encourage learners at this step to engage at least two of their peers or an entire learning team in an open dialogue about their positioning along the continuum of cultural adaptation. Do the learner's peers see him or her in the same way? Have the learner explain the justification for the positioning and then inquire with his or her peers whether his or her rationale seems reasonably thought through.

STEP 3: As a coach, suggest that one's intercultural sensitivity can be enhanced through a journey to a new culture, during which one can employ some of the interpersonal skills already covered in this chapter. There are many individual properties—some even of a moral development nature—that may predict one's depth of cultural adaptation. No matter the current level of one's intercultural competence, sensitivity can be enhanced by the degree of difference from self that one encounters in a cross-cultural journey as well as by the depth of the ensuing experience. In both instances, one's cultural framework is likely to be altered by being exposed to more complex repertoires invoking new beliefs, values, expectations, and assumptions. As learners' cognitive networks widen, their intercultural competences are likely to be enhanced.

Learners are now ready to embark on their journey. Once they have settled in, they should be informed about five generic approaches to help them reflect upon prospective engagements with people from other cultures. Learners should review each approach and try them all to get the most from their cross-cultural journey:

1. *Observation:* Once in the new cultural setting, pay attention to your surroundings and artifacts representing differences from the norms of your own culture. Examine how people address each other both verbally and nonverbally. Observe how people view you as well as what stands out as particularly unusual.

2. *Listening:* Spend time listening to others in discourse and make notes about differences in content and style of interaction. Try to focus on the challenges that people are confronting. How do they define success? Pay particular attention to how you are addressed or how people respond to you.

3. *Experimentation:* After acquiring some understanding of the new culture and developing some confidence in your own interpretative abilities, try out a limited interaction regarding a topic of personal interest. Pay particular heed to whether your experiment resulted in a mutual understanding or whether you and the other party may have "bypassed" each other (in other words, missed each other's meaning).

4. *Active involvement:* Now engage with another or the same party in a full set of exchanges as if you were from the host culture. At the same time, try to

learn more about the culture by asking some natural questions. Make sure the exchanges are not only informal and casual but that they also entail some level of serious accomplishment of mutual endeavors.

5. *Interactive involvement:* In interactive involvement, as the learner you should attempt to engage the other party (or parties) in a challenging series of discussions that could result in a new way of looking at or solving a problem. The focus is beyond a mere exchange of views; interactivity offers the opportunity for both parties to be changed as a result of the conversation.

STEP 4: In this step, learners focus on specific subjects to bring into a conversation with a party (or parties) from the new culture. An airing of these subjects should lend an appreciation of some of the critical differences between one's own and the new culture. Learners should take the stance of being totally inquisitive to the degree that any new information would be considered highly valuable to add to their multicultural repertoire.

Questions to Raise

- Could you point to some of the critical historical markers in your culture over, say, the past ten to twenty years?
- If you could change one thing about your culture, what would that be?
- How do the generations view one another in your culture?
- How is conflict viewed? How does it get resolved?
- Would you say that your culture is more individualistic or collectivistic?
- How are women viewed? Do they have equivalent rights as men? Do you believe they should have equivalent rights?
- What does it take to succeed in your culture, both in wealth and in reputation?
- Is decision making a process for everyone to participate in or is it better left to those in authority?
- In working together, is it preferable to focus on getting the job done or being sure that members are content with one another?
- How does your culture view feedback or criticism? Should either be given directly or indirectly?
- What characterizes people in your culture who have become disenfranchised or "voiceless?"

STEP 5: At the conclusion of the journey, learners reassemble their peers or learning team to debrief the journey or preferably their mutual journeys, during which time they reflect together on any critical lessons that arose for them from the experience. Prior to the dialogue, encourage learners to keep writing in their journals. Some of the questions that might be surfaced include:

- What surprised you the most from your exposure to the new culture?
- What incident or exchange particularly touched you?
- What insights have you drawn about yourself as a result of this experience?
- Where would you place yourself now on the Continuum of Cultural Adaptation?
- How would you say that the journey may have changed you?
- What did you admire about the new culture?
- What did you find most troubling or limiting about the culture?
- Do you expect to take any more journeys either of this nature or of a different nature?

Peer Coaching

Peer coaching or peer mentoring is becoming increasingly popular as a method of interpersonal development in an era when vertical ties have been replaced by horizontal ties within our organizational structures. Learners at times can more easily discuss personal feelings and insecurities with a peer coach than with a hierarchical mentor. A peer might also be particularly sensitive to diversity issues, such as race and gender, and any consequent feelings of exclusion that may arise.

If peers are to serve as coaches, they need to develop relationships that are constructive and can lead to collective reflection. In addition, learners need to develop interpersonal trust and that requires finding a peer who can work with others in a supportive and nonjudgmental way. In your role as coach, you can suggest methods to promote healthy dialogues among peer learners so that they can begin to rely more and more upon each other for productive and leaderful exchanges.

ACTIVITY 2.7

Peer Coaching Using Action Learning

This activity has been suggested by the work of Ernie Turner, president of LIM (Leadership in International Management), and relies on a variant of action learning invented by LIM known as "action reflection learning." In action learning in general, one learns from working on real-time problems occurring in one's own work environment by collaborating with peers who themselves are facing comparable problems. It is an alternative to learning from pure cognitive methods typically made available in classroom settings. It also features collective reflection on the actions taken by involving peers in focused dialogue on the problem at hand.

STEP 1: Assemble a new or existing group of learners, including perhaps some whom you personally coach. You might start by suggesting a few norms, such as that we're here to support and learn from one another using peer coaching. Participants can prepare for this meeting by thinking about a current organizational or business challenge that they would like to talk about. Once the meeting starts, the group selects one member to present his or her challenge. The group member outlines the context of the problem, its relevant history, its importance to the presenter, his or her role in the problem, what he or she has already tried, and a current question that is perplexing him or her about it. The presenter should talk through the problem in an informal way, though it would be fine to have him or her supplement the presentation by using a sketch on a flipchart or whiteboard. Give the group plenty of time to ask questions so that they are entirely familiar with the challenge being presented.

STEP 2: The peers who have just listened to the problem complete this step individually. They first pretend that the problem is theirs and write down all the questions that come to mind. During this step, they are encouraged to use the pronoun "I" instead of "you" to identify with the problem and subsequently to reduce defensiveness when they share these questions in the next step. To help stimulate the question generation, feel free to share the list of twenty great coaching questions suggested by Ernie Turner displayed in Figure 2.8. In addition, share two tips with the group that can contribute to a reduced state of defensiveness in preparing for the ensuing dialogue: (1) avoid asking questions that have a yes/no answer, and (2) avoid couching recommendations as questions in disguise. For example:

a. Instead of using a yes/no question such as, "Do you know why this challenge is important to you?"

   Consider: "Why is this challenge important to me?"

b. Instead of using a disguised question such as, "Have you talked to _____ about your problem?"

   Consider: "Whom could I talk to for support?"

The peers write down their questions on a sheet or sticky note with their name on it (in case the presenter may wish to follow up later), one sticky note

FIGURE **2.8**

Twenty Great Coaching Questions*

1. Why is this challenge important to me?

2. Whose opinions must I consider in solving this problem?

3. Who has to be involved in the solution before it will succeed?

4. What assumptions am I making that may be unfounded?

5. What are the key success factors?

6. What lessons from the past can I bring to this problem?

7. What led to this problem in the first place?

8. How did I contribute to the problem?

9. How can I contribute to the solution?

10. How can I bring others who are resisting on board?

11. What agreements do I need before I can proceed with confidence?

12. What is already working well?

13. What is pulling me and others forward?

14. What barriers are holding me and others back?

15. What supports are already in place?

16. Which stakeholders need to be consulted outside the organization?

17. What skills are required to make particular solutions work?

18. What attitudes or self-beliefs do I need in order to be successful?

19. Do I need to invest in technologies to help me solve the problem?

20. What might happen if we did nothing?

*Courtesy of Ernie Turner, president of LIM (Leadership in International Management).

per question. While this process is underway, the presenter can use the time to write down any additional questions that occur to him or her, especially ones associated with the current perplexing question surfaced at the end of the presentation.

STEP 3: Each peer, in turn, reads his or her questions and provides the presenter with the respective sticky note, without any initial comments or responses from the presenter. As the interpersonal coach, just listen to each question, but pay attention to the utterance of any "yes/no" or "disguised" questions. In these instances, gently ask the questioner to reframe the question.

STEP 4: This last step is for debriefing the presenter as well as debriefing the activity. First ask the presenter if he or she has benefited from the activity and, if so, in what ways. How does he or she view the challenge at this point? What further questions is the presenter left with? Are there any that he or she would like to discuss right now with the colleagues?

If there is time, you could replicate this activity with another individual in the group, but otherwise, focus on the experience itself. Ask everyone, not just the presenter, how they experienced this peer coaching activity. What insights did they draw from working with the presenter in the way recommended? What applications or comparable approaches may be tried in other settings? What are the implications for this team? Has it improved members' own interpersonal behavior and how they relate to one another?

Finally, it should be noted that this peer coaching activity can be replicated virtually. Simply have a focal team member e-mail a challenge to his or her peer coaches, requesting their questions within a specific deadline.

CASE STUDY

"Hiring the Temporaries": A Case Using the Left-Hand Column

PHILIP MCARTHUR

Background

Karen Jones was the director of an operating unit in a large financial institution. Like many managers today, she understood the limits of the "heroic leader" model and the importance of engaging the collective intelligence of her team to deal with the complex challenges they faced. Although she aspired to being a "leaderful" manager, she had a tendency to become impatient and overly controlling, particularly when team members resisted her suggestions or made recommendations she found problematic. She wanted to involve her group in making decisions and building consensus, when possible, but she was the one who would be held accountable for results, and she didn't have time for protracted debates.

The Situation

A costly staffing decision exemplified Karen's contradictory management approach. Her operating unit had been experiencing a high degree of absenteeism and turnover. Meanwhile, work deadlines were being missed and customers were complaining. Karen believed a solution needed to be implemented quickly, and to her it was obvious: hire temporary workers to help with the work backlog until the company could hire permanent employees. She met with one of her supervisors and proposed the idea. To her surprise, the supervisor disagreed and said that hiring temporary workers would exacerbate the problem. However, under Karen's pressure, he relented and agreed to hire the "temporaries." Unfortunately, he was right. Fixing the errors made by the temporaries added to the deadline problems and drove up costs.

Karen was highly motivated to understand how she had contributed to this problematic decision. She wrote out her conversation with the supervisor using the Left-Hand Column activity (Activity 2.2) described earlier in this chapter. In the right-hand column, Karen wrote down what she and the supervisor actually said. In the left-hand column she wrote what she was thinking and feeling that she did not say (see Table 2.3).

The Intervention

My Theoretical Approach

In my coaching work, I help people reflect on their "behavioral footprint"—how they characteristically think, feel, and act in high-stakes situations—so that they are able to create the results they want. When people have difficult conversations, there is often a gap, of which they are unaware, between their intentions and their actions. Writing a left-hand column case enables you to discover such gaps. For Karen, like most managers we have worked with, becoming aware of an inconsistency between deeply held values ("be open and collaborative") and her actual behavior was a strong motivator for change.

As the Left-Hand Column case illustrates, in difficult conversations there are actually two conversations happening simultaneously: the public conversation that everyone is aware of (the right-hand column) and the private conversation

TABLE **2.2**

Karen's Difficult Conversation

What I Thought and Felt	What We Actually Said
We've got to address this problem immediately. I have a solution that I hope the supervisor will agree to implement.	Me: We need to use temporary staff until we can hire permanent employees and clean up the backlog.
	Supervisor: Temporaries won't help. They don't understand our work and will make our problems worse.
This is so frustrating. Supervisors aren't willing to risk trying something different. But I don't want to appear closed-minded.	Me: Okay, I'm open to suggestions. How should we deal with this situation?
	Supervisor: We just need to tough it out by working overtime and weekends. Eventually this situation will sort itself out.
I'm getting really mad! This solution won't work. The overtime necessary to fix it will burn out our employees. Why can't he see that!?	Me: If we don't do something different, we will lose customers and management support before this thing gets fixed.
Now we're getting someplace!	Supervisor: Okay, okay! Let's hire the temporaries.

(the left-hand column) in each person's head. You can either allow your left-hand column to sabotage you (as it did Karen), or use it as a resource to help you stay on a productive track. I use a number of tools to help my clients diagnose inconsistencies between their intentions and actions and between their public and private conversations.

Together, for example, we reflect on both the balance and quality of their advocacy and inquiry—as is demonstrated in Activity 2.2. When people advocate a point of view, they often "jump to conclusions" (or, as we say in my consulting practice, "jump up a ladder of inference") rather than make the steps in their reasoning explicit. This makes it difficult to discover limits in each others' thinking. Additionally, people tend to discourage others from questioning their thinking and consequently are not seen as open to influence. When we do ask questions, we typically ask either "closed" questions (which can be answered yes or no but don't elicit someone's reasoning), or rhetorical questions, which are advocacy disguised as inquiry and are experienced as manipulative.

Reflecting on Karen's Public Conversation

In Karen's case, I helped her see that her conversation with the supervisor involved almost all advocacy—on both their parts—and that the quality of their advocacy was low. They both state their conclusions but neither of them explains the steps in their thinking. Given this, there are many questions they could have asked each other to make a better-informed decision. For example, Karen could ask the supervisor how he understands the cause of the absenteeism and turnover, what his experience has been with temporary workers, how he thinks they will make the problem worse, and how he assesses the risks and costs of hiring them versus the risks and costs of other possible solutions. These questions would require the supervisor to "come down his ladder." Instead, Karen asks, "How should we deal with the situation?" While an "open" question, it is not a useful question. Rather than enabling Karen to understand the supervisor's concerns, her question leads him to "go back up his ladder" and state conclusions she sees as unrealistic. At this point she loses patience, stops asking questions, and pressures the supervisor to do what she wants. The conversation results in a win-lose competition, rather than an opportunity for learning and collaboration.

Reflecting on Karen's Left-Hand Column

After helping Karen see what was problematic about her behavior, we reflected on what led her to act as she did. The interaction with the supervisor (advocating their conclusions, not explaining their reasoning, not asking each other useful questions, discouraging challenge) is not accidental or random. It is common in difficult conversations and is shaped by a mindset (a set of underlying values, assumptions, and beliefs) that we find illustrated in her left-hand column. For example, given Karen's mindset about the supervisor ("Supervisors aren't willing to risk trying something different"), it's not surprising she neither encouraged questions about her view nor asked questions about his concerns. She was not thinking, "Perhaps he is right. I wonder what he sees that I don't?" Instead, she dismissed his concerns as indicating a character flaw of supervisors in general.

In difficult conversations, when people create undesired results, often it is not because they have bad intentions. Rather, they have conflicting intentions that put them in a bind. The Left-Hand Column activity provides useful data to help understand these dilemmas. For example, in Karen's left-hand column, we see that while she dismisses the supervisor's concerns, she also believes that a manager should be collaborative and open-minded. Consequently, rather than inquire into his thinking (which she has dismissed), she professes that she is open and asks for an alternative solution. Unfortunately, it is hard to sustain inquiry when your mindset is not one of curiosity and you have already dismissed the other person's view. You can say you are open, but when your thinking is closed it will show in your actions—usually as soon as the other person disagrees. Any leaderful impulse becomes squashed in practice.

To change the way that we talk with others, we need to change the way that we talk to ourselves. For example, when the supervisor gave in to Karen's pressure at the end of their conversation, Karen's left-hand column was, "Now we are getting someplace!" After reviewing her case, she had a key insight:

> "In the future, whenever I prevail in a tough conversation and hear myself say to myself, 'Now we are getting someplace!' I won't be relieved. I'll be worried. I'll realize I am getting someplace—I'm probably getting myself in trouble!"

Recrafting Karen's Dialogue: New Mindset, New Actions, New Results

After helping Karen understand how she became stuck in her conversation with the supervisor, our next step was to discuss how she could think and act differently. First, I asked her what new results she would hope to achieve in at least three domains: the tasks she wanted to accomplish, the issues she would need to learn about in order to accomplish the tasks, and the relationship she wanted to build. Explicitly imagining the results you want to create helps you orient yourself to the mindset and actions necessary to achieve them. In Karen's case, her task was to decide how to address the work backlog and how to resolve the unit's long- and short-term staffing problems. To achieve this she needed to learn the underlying causes of the turnover and absenteeism, to generate solutions for the staffing problem and the work backlog, and to assess the risks and costs of the various options. She also wanted to build a relationship with the supervisor in which both felt understood and respected by the other and committed to taking action.

Once she identified her desired results, the next step was to ask her to do a thought experiment—to imagine a mindset that would enable her to act differently. Her initial mindset, reflected in both her left-hand column and in her behavior, was that her solution was obviously correct, the supervisor's concerns were unreasonable, and that her task was to convince him that she was right. Through coaching, she was able to compose a set of new assumptions to test:

- I have a perspective but can't see everything.
- The supervisor may see things that I miss, and, in his mind, is acting sensibly.

- My purpose is to make the best choice, not convince the supervisor I am right.
- Our inability to act collaboratively is more about skill than motive; if we get stuck, I may be contributing in ways I am unaware of. If so, I need to learn.

From this productive mindset, Karen invented a set of new actions that would make it difficult for the supervisor to respond in his typical way, and more likely he would respond in ways Karen would find helpful. She imagined the following set of actions, which combined both high-quality advocacy and inquiry:

1. Frame the purpose of the conversation and suggest a process to address the issues.
2. Explain how I see the problem; make the steps in my thinking explicit.
3. Invite questions and comments from the supervisor about my thinking; inquire into his reasoning, interests, and concerns.
4. If we get stuck, ask the supervisor what I am doing that is not helpful.

Having invented a new mindset and actions, it was important for Karen to test her ideas. I asked her to go through several iterations of the conversation with me to ensure she was able to put her new ideas into practice. Ultimately, she was able to develop a more constructive approach, with a beginning to her conversation with her supervisor as illustrated:

> "I'd like to discuss how we can address our problems with absenteeism and turnover and how to clear up our work backlog. I suggest we start by discussing the underlying causes of both sets of problems and make sure we have a shared view. Then we can generate solution options and assess the risks and costs of each one. I want us to be committed to whatever we decide together, so let's make sure we address all of our doubts and concerns. Before we start, let me check—what questions or thoughts do you have about the agenda I've suggested?"

Chapter Three

Team-Level Change

TEAM-LEVEL CHANGE IS OFTEN MANIFESTED THROUGH the vehicle of the learning team, in which time is dedicated not necessarily to the task at hand but to individual and group learning. The change agent, who assists in this learning process, shall be referred to here as the "facilitator." A facilitator can be the appointed supervisor of the group, a member within the group, or a consultant from outside the group. The facilitator's primary role initially is to raise awareness of the natural dynamics of groups and organizations so that group members may realize the challenge but also the benefit of mutually developing their team.

If the facilitator is the official team leader, he or she might suggest to the community that leadership can become shared as long as everyone is willing to pitch in to "cover" the leadership of the team. During the early development phase, this individual may need to assume some of the functions associated with standard supervision: calling meetings, setting an agenda, coordinating tasks and schedules, and the like.

Once members become more comfortable with the notion of sharing leadership, they can begin to see the value of distributing a variety of leadership roles and functions among themselves. Gradually, the facilitator or facilitative supervisor may exhibit more leaderful behaviors, such as encouraging members to take risks and even to fail, coaching them on active listening, providing nondefensive feedback, acknowledging emotions, or valuing differences.

The six activities in this chapter are designed to help change agents perfect their facilitating skills and also to use these skills to develop a more leaderful team.

The first activity, **Learning to Facilitate**, encourages intervention in an ongoing team to try out some new facilitative skills. Possible interventions are fully listed along with relevant examples.

The second activity, **The Pilot and the Mountaineer**, helps you as a facilitator discover the value of engaging team members in what is called "concurrent leadership," which allows them to bring out their respective leadership skills to help the team with its task and maintenance functions.

The third activity, **The Ned Wicker Case**, demonstrates the need and the means to develop a team to a point at which its members might be prepared to take over the leadership of the team as a collective responsibility.

The fourth activity, **Team Member Leadership Roles**, asks your team members to identify their leadership role strengths that can be offered to help the team in its mission; members are also invited to use their role analysis, with the team's assistance, to develop any underdeveloped leadership skills.

The fifth activity, **Mapping the Continuum of Leaderful Team Development**, focuses on team development, whereby team members collectively dialogue on where the team stands in its evolution toward leaderful practice.

The sixth activity, **Team Reflective Practice for Self-Renewal**, takes advantage of emerging facilitation skills to ask the team to pause and reflect on any opportunities to improve the team by managing any issues that may be impeding its growth.

Facilitative Skills

Activity 3.1 is designed to develop one's facilitation skills by reviewing the guidelines for facilitators depicted in Table 3.1. The guidelines provide a set of recommendations for engaging a team, the members of which are concerned about learning. Specific examples of each of the recommended behaviors are provided in the right-hand side of the table.

TABLE **3.1**

Some Guidelines for Facilitators

Recommendation	Example
Try to remain nonjudgmental and at the same time empathic.	Don't immediately evaluate others' ideas Wholeheartedly support those who offer new ideas.
Be courteous and fair and give everyone a chance to speak.	Be careful not to endorse anyone's ideas over others' by saying something innocent but biased, such as, "That's a good idea."
Move to establish ground rules, such as:	Only one person speaks at a time. All personal accounts stay within the group. Everyone shares in making the conversation productive.
Manage time so that everyone gets a chance to be the focus of attention.	You could say, "Thanks Sue; if you think we've covered your issue sufficiently, might we go on now to Jim?"
Encourage members to speak freely, express new ideas, and register dissent.	"I appreciate your willingness to state an alternative point of view, Rick."
Shift focus when too much attention has been dedicated to only one person or idea.	"We've been focusing on this proposal for a while. Would anyone like to offer another?"
Show sensitivity to cultural differences.	Ask whether particular styles are familiar given one's cultural background. For example, is it acceptable to voice one's emotions?
Be patient and don't interrupt or finish others' sentences.	Allow and even encourage occasional silence.
Display active listening, using paraphrasing or perception checking.	"Let me see, if I am hearing you correctly. . . . "
Try not to become the central reference point.	Redirect questions so that members can interact among each other. Don't feel a need to comment after each person speaks.
Check out your assumptions and ask others to do the same.	"I assume that you're speaking on behalf of Glen's proposal. Is that correct?"

(Continued on next page)

TABLE **3.1**   *(Continued)*

Recommendation	Example
Don't suppress conflict; recognize and manage it, but keep it focused on the issue, not on the person	You could ask, for example, "What can we do to work together on this even though we may not agree?"
Accept deep emotions and try to work with them	"May I ask why you feel so strongly about this issue?"
Ask for clarification and zero in on points made to get at people's reasoning	"I think I understand your point, but can you tell us how you have come to your conclusions?"
Model personal inquiry by asking nondefensive questions, such as:	Could you give an illustration of that point?
	How do you respond to some of the concerns that have been expressed?
	How has your thinking changed about the issues(s) at hand?
	What do others think about this point?
Probe into the team's process using reflective questions	How do you think we have done in handling this issue?
	What have you heard today that has touched you in some way?
	What ideas have not been expressed?
	Who's been left out of our deliberations whom we should hear from?
	Can we identify any sense of shared purpose?
	What have we learned from this process?
Ask, when appropriate, if it would be worthwhile to summarize important points or decisions	Should we take a moment now to summarize our key points or conclusions?
Ask if the group wishes to use some supportive roles to facilitate the group process	Should the group appoint someone to serve as a recorder?
	Should the group appoint someone as an observer for a particular discussion?

ACTIVITY 3.1

Learning to Facilitate

This activity invites prospective facilitators to intervene in their teams and then follows up by asking team members to fill out a feedback sheet to help point facilitators to areas that were relatively effective in moving the team toward greater collective leadership.

STEP 1: Request the opportunity to provide facilitation to any group of which you are a member (unless, of course, you are already a facilitator). If this is your first attempt at process—as opposed to content—facilitation, perhaps ask initially for merely a half-hour (or preferably one hour) during which you would attempt to make selective interventions like the recommended strategies in Table 3.1. Since process facilitation tends to feature passive over active intervention, don't force the issue; just add your comments when deemed advisable.

STEP 2: After your facilitated segment, pass out the feedback sheet, see Figure 3.1, next page, and request the team members to fill it out. Study and reflect upon this feedback at your leisure.

STEP 3: As the feedback sheets are being collected, ask the team members to provide further comments to you verbally.

....

FIGURE **3.1**

Feedback Sheet for Facilitator

Now that your facilitator has completed his or her opportunity to serve the team in a facilitative capacity, could you help by answering the following questions and passing the sheet back to your facilitator? Your frank responses will help this facilitator learn to improve in this role. You needn't answer any questions that did not apply during this occasion.

1. The session improved in its effectiveness as a result of the facilitation (please circle one).

	To a great extent	To a moderate extent	Somewhat	Not at all
	4	3	2	1

a. If the session improved, what specifically did the facilitator do to assist the team?

b. Do you recall any specific interventions by the facilitator that were helpful? Not helpful?

c. If the session did not improve, did the facilitator do anything to hold the team back? If so, what specifically would you point to?

2. The facilitator was helpful to me.

	To a great extent	To a moderate extent	Somewhat	Not at all
	4	3	2	1

a. How was the facilitator helpful to you?

(Continued on next page)

FIGURE **3.1**   *(Continued)*

3. The facilitator was helpful to other group members.

	To a great extent	To a moderate extent	Somewhat	Not at all
	4	3	2	1

a. With whom and how was the facilitator helpful to others?

4. The facilitator helped the group learn.

	To a great extent	To a moderate extent	Somewhat	Not at all
	4	3	2	1

a. Can you cite any specific instances?

5. The facilitator helped me or other individual group members learn.

	To a great extent	To a moderate extent	Somewhat	Not at all
	4	3	2	1

a. Can you cite any specific instances?

6. The facilitator helped the team manage conflict.

	To a great extent	To a moderate extent	Somewhat	Not at all
	4	3	2	1

a. Can you cite any specific instances?

(Continued on next page)

FIGURE **3.1**   *(Continued)*

7. The facilitator helped the team face some deep emotions.

	To a great extent	To a moderate extent	Somewhat	Not at all
	4	3	2	1

a. Can you cite any specific instances?

8. The facilitator helped the team by encouraging all to express their ideas freely, even if outside the norm.

	To a great extent	To a moderate extent	Somewhat	Not at all
	4	3	2	1

a. Can you cite any specific instances?

9. The facilitator modeled for the team how to be a sensitive team member.

	To a great extent	To a moderate extent	Somewhat	Not at all
	4	3	2	1

a. Can you point to what he or she did that revealed a degree of sensitivity?

10. Are there any other attributes of the facilitator that you would like to mention, either positive or negative?

Concurrent Leadership

Although the prescription for concurrent self-directed leadership is clear in theory (one could cite the need for resilient leadership in organizations that have to operate globally with responsive service and product lines or the popular use of self-directed groups among our top public companies), it is not as easy to implement. What makes it so difficult is a view that if one is not "leading," he or she is potentially abdicating responsibility—not to mention that the person with authority in the group may feel that his or her very authority would be usurped if exerted by anyone else. The leaderful perspective that leadership may emerge from anyone in the group at any time is simply a radical proposition in our culture of individualistic (rather than collective) leadership.

Consider the instance of Sir Ernest Shackleton, renowned Antarctic explorer, known more these days for his portentous leadership practices. Consider how he recruited for his voyages. He wanted recruits who could complement their technical skills with such important attributes as a team spirit, optimism, and a pleasing, even humorous, disposition. But when it came to the need for expertise, Shackleton was quick to hire on people who had all the technical skills that he lacked. Not only was he not at all intimidated by their superior education and expertise, he encouraged them to extend their learning however they saw fit.

....

ACTIVITY 3.2

The Pilot and the Mountaineer

In order to appreciate the value of concurrent leadership, read The Pilot and the Mountaineer Case below. Then, be prepared to move on to the succeeding steps, most of which are questions for reflection on the case. Although the material is directed to you as a facilitator, you may also wish to share the case and its reflections with any of your teams, the members of which may be interested in leaderful practice.

The Pilot and the Mountaineer Case

A bomber team was in the last stages of training. The crew had performed well and had developed a close working as well as a personal relationship with one another. Contributing to their success was the pilot, who was the head of the team but who was also well liked and respected, not only as a pilot but as a person. Another factor in their success was that all but one member of the team came from urban areas of the country and had much in common. During off-duty hours, they would go to local bars, have a few beers, and recount tall tales of their deeds back home. One of the team members, however, an enlisted man, was a social isolate. He came from the mountains of West Virginia, was unacquainted with urban life, and because of his religious upbringing chose not to join the team during their bar-hopping activities, which also included playing cards, dancing, and drinking. So when the team got together off-duty, he was usually absent. He preferred to spend time reading his Bible and e-mailing his parents and girlfriend back home.

At one point, the team had to go on survival training. They were dropped by helicopter into the middle of the Canadian Rockies with a minimum of equipment and needed to find their way back to civilization.

In this situation, the mountaineer from West Virginia was in his element. The weather was cold and rainy, but he was able to find dry moss and bark to start fires. For food, he could wade in mountain streams and reach down to feel for trout with his bare hands and then flip them onto the bank of the stream. Seeing what he was capable of doing, the other team members began to develop new respect for him. They, along with the pilot, decided to follow his suggestions and, in due course, the team passed their survival test with flying colors.

STEP 1: Your first question—to answer by yourself and then in discussion with colleagues—is, who is the "leader" of this group?

The question, as it turns out, is a trick question, because there is more than one leader. Both the pilot and the mountaineer are leaders.

STEP 2: Is it possible for the pilot and the mountaineer to be leading at the same time? To respond to this question, let's consider a concept called "base of power," initially proposed by John R. P. French Jr. and Bertram Raven.[9] French and Raven advanced the view that there can be many bases of power—assuming *power* is the ability of any individual to get others to do something. Defined in this way, most of us might accept the proposition that power is intrinsically connected to the practice of leadership.

Consider, then, eight different bases of power:

1. *Coercive power*, through forcing others to do something
2. *Connection power*, through one's contacts and networks

---

[9] J. R. P. French Jr. and B. Raven, "The Bases of Social Power," pp. 607–623 in D. Cartwright and A. Zander, eds., *Group Dynamics* (New York: Harper and Row, 1960).

3. *Reward power*, from any pecuniary or nonpecuniary benefits that could be extended to others

4. *Legitimate power*, through position, rank, or authority

5. *Charismatic power*, from one's pleasing disposition or personality

6. *Information power*, from the ability to amass the necessary information or resources to help the group

7. *Expert power*, from one's existing knowledge that can be applied to the situation at hand

8. *Meaning-making power*, from the meaning that someone could offer to help the group understand its identity as it works through its problems

So, what are the respective bases of power of the pilot and the mountaineer?

The pilot clearly has legitimate power based upon his authority or legitimate position, but he also happens to have charismatic power based on his personality. The mountaineer also exhibits leadership due to his expert power.

STEP 3: Do you consider the pilot to have been an effective leader during the survival training experience? If so, why?

It is noteworthy that the pilot seems to have recognized the leadership offered by the mountaineer in this situation and clearly did not hold him back for fear of his usurping the pilot's authority. Have you ever seen a situation in which supervisors, upon recognizing someone's expertise, might ask the expert to inform them first so that they can uphold their authority and tell the group?

STEP 4: Did the pilot give up his authority during survival training?

The pilot appears to have not only retained his authority but may have subtly (or perhaps even ostensibly) used it to support the interventions of the mountaineer.

STEP 5: Are there opportunities for members of any of your facilitated teams to share leadership, like the pilot did in this instance? Are there opportunities for a supervisor of one of your teams to share leadership? If your current supervisor is not willing to share leadership, what might be blocking him or her from doing so? Can you play a productive role in helping this supervisor remove some of these roadblocks?

Having completed your review of this case, feel free now to share it with your teams as a provocation to a robust dialogue on the value of and constraints against concurrent leadership.

Situational Development

One of the roles of a facilitator is to help teams reach a stage of leaderful self-direction. There are many normative models from the field of group dynamics that facilitators can consult both to diagnose team processes and to responsively intervene in their teams. For example, in one model facilitators intervene based upon whether the problem under consideration has to do with effort, task performance, knowledge and skills, or group processes. If the level of effort or motivation is insufficient, the facilitator (or facilitating member) might have the group reflect upon its behavioral norms. If, for example, members have adopted a so-called preferred value norm of just doing what it takes to get the job done but no more than that, then the group may need to engage in a dialogue about what might be preventing members from trying to achieve at a higher level. If there is a problem with task performance, one option might be to reconsider the design of the work team itself. Perhaps subgroups might be formed to accomplish work that formerly had to wait until the full team was assembled.

The situational model of leadership, initially applied to one-on-one manager-subordinate interactions by Paul H. Hersey and Kenneth H. Blanchard,[10] has been adapted for purposes of group development by Don Carew, Eunice Parisi-Carew, and Ken Blanchard.[11] Accordingly, facilitators might deploy different degrees of two principal behaviors in their work in groups. First is *task behavior*, which is relatively directive to the members regarding their roles and assignments and what they need to do to accomplish the work of the team. The second principal behavior, *maintenance behavior*, provides support and encouragement to group members, facilitating their interaction and involving them in decision making.

We know from situational leadership that leaders can adapt their style to fit the situation. Hence, a proper combination of task and maintenance behaviors is advised depending upon the stage of development of the team in question. In effect, the facilitator can help move a group through four stages of a group's life. The four stages to be considered here—forming, storming, norming, and performing—were initially developed by B. Tuckman[12] and

---

[10] P. Hersey and K. H. Blanchard, *Management of Organizational Behavior*, 5th ed. (Upper Saddle River, NJ: Prentice-Hall, 1988).

[11] D. Carew, E. Parisi-Carew, and K. Blanchard, *Group Development and Situational Leadership II* (Escondido, CA: Blanchard Training and Development, Inc., 1990).

[12] B. Tuckman, "Development Sequence in Small Groups," *Psychological Bulletin*, 63, pp. 348–399, 1965.

may be described in terms of the amount of work expected from each stage as well as the morale or socioemotional tone of the group. The amount of work accomplished steadily increases through the stages. Morale starts out high during the forming stage but then takes a dip during the storming stage as the expectations of the members confront the stern reality of trying to reach a high level of task performance without having worked through the requisite conflict management and norm development functions. As norms are clarified in this and the subsequent stage, morale begins to pick up until it reaches a high level in the performing stage.

Table 3.2 depicts the four stages, the relative degree of task and maintenance behavior advised for each stage, and the leadership style recommended for the facilitator.

At the first or *forming* stage of group development, the "telling" style is most appropriate as the team struggles to clarify its task and to set realistic and attainable goals. Telling stipulates a low level of maintenance behavior, just enough to establish a climate for member acceptance of one another and to introduce the process goals of open communication and shared leadership. The telling style may require facilitators to inform the team about its own development so that members can understand cognitively what may evolve as the team matures. Facilitators may also need to help members gradually open up to one another in deciding on agendas for meetings, on plans for action, on developing a system for documentation, on distributing workloads and roles, and on determining critical success factors.

By the second or *storming* stage of group development, the facilitator is seen as having to increase the level of maintenance behavior to balance

TABLE **3.2**

Situational Team Leadership and Group Development

Stage	Task Behavior	Maintenance Behavior	Style
Forming	High	Low	*Telling*
Storming	High	High	*Coaching*
Norming	Low	Moderate	*Joining*
Performing	Low	Low	*Delegating*

task provision. Essentially, a "coaching" style is called for as the facilitator guides team members in the skills and knowledge associated with task performance and group process. The goal at this stage is to work toward less dependency on the facilitator and more self-sufficiency within the group. This may entail such task behaviors as pointing out concealed problems, be they overexpenditures or portentous trends; broadening the group's repertoire of problem-solving skills or quality tools; making suggestions about performance improvements; disseminating companywide information important to the group; or providing informal rewards or reinforcement when the group assumes responsibility for its own tasks. Coaching also delves into process behaviors such as modeling active listening, showing concern for team members' well-being, acknowledging and managing interpersonal difficulties and natural conflicts that arise among team members, and focusing on building supportive member relationships and group cohesion. During this stage in team development, certain members may see themselves as "natural leaders" and prematurely attempt to take over the group. Others in the team may perceive this type of behavior as presumptive or even as coercive. Although the facilitator needs to allow some of these dynamics to play out on their own, he or she needs to ensure that they indeed get played out. This may require the facilitator to encourage some of the quieter members to voice their concerns about unchecked controlling behavior on the part of the more vocal or assertive members. In coaching, what the facilitator is attempting to do is not to stifle the natural energy among the vocal members as much as guide them to listen to others and help them reflect on their operating behavior.

The "joining" style aligns with the *norming* or third stage, during which the facilitator significantly diminishes emphasis on task and goal clarification. The facilitator at this stage encourages group members to assume more and more of the maintenance functions that were once his or her province. As this stage evolves, the facilitator applies only moderate maintenance behavior as group members begin to assume more discretion regarding process dynamics. However, the facilitator needs to be alert to an inclination on the part of some members to avoid conflict and disagreement for fear of losing their newfound cohesion. The facilitator needs to encourage continued free expression, balanced participation, and valuing of differences among members.

In the final *performing* stage, the facilitator uses a "delegating" style as the group itself begins to take responsibility for task and maintenance functions. Although the facilitator continues to monitor the goals and performance of the group, he or she can become more of a resource for individuals and for the group as a whole—for example, in providing technical support for members' projects. The facilitator also has to be aware of the need, as the occasion arises, to become more involved if conditions in the team were to change—for example, if new members were to join the team or if a crisis, such as the loss of a key client, were to occur. This may also be a point during which the group may need some assistance in preparing for its possible dissolution.

It goes without saying that although leaderful practice is ecumenical in its approach, it does endorse the need to develop teams along situational lines. Thus a facilitator must be sufficiently adroit to be able to deploy each of the four styles, with an expectation that in due course, you will be able to use joining and delegating approaches as your predominant modus operandi.

....

ACTIVITY 3.3

The Ned Wicker Case

To obtain a sense about how to use the situational development model, first read the Ned Wicker case study to follow. The case takes place in a high-tech company department that has assembled a high-skilled staff of talented engineers to bid on government proposals. The manager of the department, Ned Wicker, exhibits leadership behavior that appears to eventually lead to a problematic outcome. The steps after the case should inspire some reflection on the reader's part regarding Ned's need for control that short-circuits the team's leaderful development. In addition to the case's contribution to your own development as a facilitator, feel free to share the entire activity with a team you're facilitating to promote a deeper understanding of the link between situational and leaderful development.

The Ned Wicker Case*

Ned Wicker is a new manager of the Systems Proposal Department of the Graubart Chemtronics Company. The department had been recently organized to coordinate efforts by the company to gain new nanotech business using its patented silicone technology. Its specific functions were to:

1. Carefully review and evaluate all incoming government bid specifications for new compounds required by EPA and other users of such technology

---

*This case was adapted from an original case taking place in the electronics industry written by Prof. John W. Lewis III of Boston College, Chestnut Hill, Massachusetts.

2. Decide which of the bids (if any) would be potentially profitable within both the technical and manufacturing capabilities of Graubart

3. Prepare the necessary proposals to win contracts from primarily governmental customers

In the high-tech industry in particular, skillful bidding is critical. If the bid is too high, it rarely nets the business, but if it's too low ("buying" the contract), it may get bled by the job.

Ned had been a senior proposal analyst with another company when he was hired by the president of Graubart to set up the new department. The new job coincided with his completion of an MBA, which he obtained a few years after graduating magna cum laude from Penn State with a chemical engineering degree. This job was also Ned's first managerial position. He personally recruited and hired a diverse group of seven highly qualified engineers as systems proposal analysts, most of whom had prior experience with customer requirements in the industry. The president of Graubart, Ned's boss, was enthusiastic about the new group, especially Ned's hands-on approach in getting things organized and underway.

Since the work of generating and submitting technical proposals for potential customers can be both costly and time consuming, Ned felt the key to his department's success would be the careful preliminary screening and selection of bid possibilities on which proposals were to be prepared by the group. It was largely for this reason that he built such an elite team of professionals to work with him, and he developed a procedure for full participation by the entire team in the RFP (request for proposal) selection process. (An RFP is the means by which a potential supplier invites bids for contract work.)

Ned's preliminary procedure called for all RFPs to be distributed and given a preliminary evaluation by the individual analysts, who then would make informal written "bid-no bid" recommendations to him on Friday each week. On Mondays, a full morning review meeting involving the entire team would be held, at which time each analyst would present in detail those proposals he or she had reviewed the preceding week and moderate a group discussion about them. After all RFPs had been reviewed in this way, final selections for making proposals were to be reached by group consensus.

The RFP review and selection procedure seemed to work effectively for the first three or four months, and three proposals submitted by the department resulted in major new contracts for the company. Discussions in the Monday morning review meetings about various RFPs were lively and involved the whole group. Frequently the sessions ran over into the early afternoon. The variety of individual backgrounds, consciously selected by Ned, provided the team with a broad technical perspective for approaching its task. On only two occasions, based on strategic information he had gained from top management staff meetings, did Ned find it necessary to overrule the group's decisions. This was not done high-handedly, however, and Ned was able to convince members about the wisdom of this final decision.

At the Monday meeting following the announcement of the second contract won by the team, the president paid a surprise visit just before lunch with a bottle of champagne for Ned and the team to show his appreciation for their efforts to date.

While Ned was pleased with the quality of the decisions made by the team during the first months, two things began to bother him. Although the number of proposals being reviewed remained about the same, each successive week, the Monday morning meetings seemed to last longer and would soon consume the entire day, a luxury he felt the department couldn't afford. He also had a nagging feeling that as the manager, he needed to be better prepared to discuss the merits of the RFPs in order to assist the group in reaching the soundest decisions.

Since he received the written recommendations on Fridays, he decided to familiarize himself with them over the weekend and to arrive at his own tentative conclusions and priorities for making a bid-no bid decision for each RFP. His purpose was to have answers ready, which might speed up group discussion on Mondays, but to do so in a way that did not directly influence members of the team as to his tentative conclusions.

Except for his having less time for golf and weekend household chores, this additional effort by Ned seemed to bear results. And although the team's batting average for successful proposals declined in the second quarter, he felt better prepared on Monday morning, and the meetings began to shorten with discussions more to the point. This had the dual advantage of enabling the team to handle a larger number of proposals in the meetings and also freed up valuable time for the analysts to do the ongoing work of the department.

A disquieting thing began to develop, however. Gradually, discussions in the team became more formal, and at times, became an exchange between Ned and the analyst who had done the preliminary evaluation. The final blow came this morning, when the meeting lasted a mere forty-five minutes with Ned doing most of the talking. Since he considered this review meeting to be the heart of the RFP selection process, Ned became alarmed. While he still had complete confidence in the professionals he had selected, he felt more and more that in the review meetings, they were holding back their ideas and technical judgment, both of which he knew were crucial to arriving at the soundest bid-no bid decisions.

As he mulled over the situation on his way to lunch, one of the analysts in the team who had received the second highest performance rating stopped Ned to say he was leaving to take a position elsewhere.

STEP 1: Please review the continuum displayed in Figure 3.2. In it four leadership styles are depicted:

1. *Tell:* The manager tells the team what to do.
2. *Sell/Coach:* The manager explains how to do the task.
3. *Join/Support:* The manager participates with the team in conducting the job.

FIGURE **3.2**

The Four-Style Leadership Continuum*

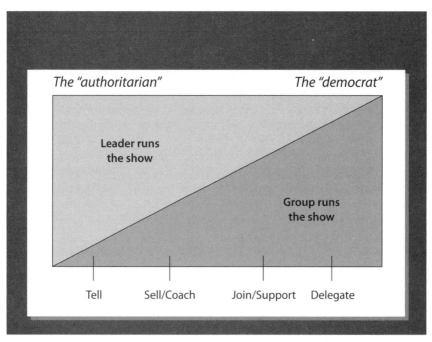

*Adapted from The Continuum of Leadership Behavior in R. Tannenbaum & W. H. Schmidt, "How to Choose a Leadership Pattern," *Harvard Business Review,* May-June, 1973. Granted by permission, Harvard Business School Publishing.

4. *Delegate:* The manager turns the task and decisions about the task over to the team.

Where would you place Ned Wicker's team leadership style at the beginning of the case and at the end of the case?

STEP 2: Indeed, Ned drifted over to the left side of the continuum, probably even to the left of sell/coach. Was this an effective shift? If not, why not? How would you respond to Ned's concern that the meetings were taking too long?

STEP 3: Given that Ned had been successful as a join/support leader to begin with, how could he have brought up his concern about meeting length and stayed with his erstwhile effective style?

STEP 4: What was it about the members of this team and its development from the outset through Ned's efforts that predisposed it to a more collaborative style?

STEP 5: Do you believe that this team could benefit from having Ned delegate full responsibility to it; if so, would Ned have worked himself out of a job?

....

Leadership Roles

Meredith Belbin, in *Management Teams*,[13] discusses the responsibility that team members have to perform a variety of team roles: setting priorities, using resources wisely, advancing new ideas, fostering team spirit, completing tasks, and the like. As team members begin to assume more of these roles and rely less on the supervisor, team leadership becomes within reach.

....

ACTIVITY 3.4

Team Member Leadership Roles

Consider the steps in this activity as a way to understand some of the many roles that can be filled as part of a team's overall leadership. Some of the roles may be only emergent but may be fulfilled not only as a means to help the team but to also help individual team members learn.

---

[13] R. M. Belbin, *Management Teams: Why They Succeed or Fail* (New York: Wiley, 1981).

TABLE **3.3**

Belbin's Team Roles*

Belbin's Roles	Definition
• shaper	Sets objectives and shapes the way team effort is applied; establishes a pattern for group processes and outcomes
• implementor	Turns concepts and goals into practical working procedures; carries out plans conscientiously
• coordinator	Sees that the best use is made of the team's resources; recognizes the strengths and weaknesses of team members
• completer-finisher	Protects the team from mistakes of commission and omission; searches for aspects that need greater attention; sees that work gets done consistently
• monitor-evaluator	Analyzes problems and evaluates ideas and suggestions seriously so that the team is positioned to make balanced decisions
• team worker	Supports and enables team members; provides an informal network of communication beyond the team's formal activities
• plant	Advances new ideas and strategies; looks for new or even radical ways to approach problems
• resource investigator	Explores and reports on ideas, developments, and resources often outside the group
• specialist	Provides knowledge and skills in rare supply and often contributes a professional viewpoint

*With permission of Belbin Associates © e-interplace, Belbin Associates, UK.

STEP 1: Refer your team members to Belbin's roles, depicted in Table 3.3. Each role is defined.

STEP 2: Ask each member to assess his or her primary role strength. Which of the nine roles does he or she think he or she performs most often in the group?

STEP 3: Ask each member to select a secondary role strength.

STEP 4: Ask each member to reveal his or her role priorities and then initiate a feedback discussion—one member at a time—to determine whether members agree with the individual's selection. If there is disagreement on the role priorities, the feedback discussion should turn to the identification of alternative role strengths that particular members bring to the team. Keep track of the allocation of role responsibilities—self- and other-nominated.

STEP 5: Moderate a team dialogue on which roles are well represented by team members and which represent current gaps in the team's leadership. Then, entertain a discussion about which roles—currently undersupplied—could be fulfilled by which members. Continue the discussion regarding which roles members would like to try to take on, as a learning goal, whether or not it represents a current gap in the team's leadership.

Leaderful Team Development

Just as teams evolve at varying rates toward fuller development, they also require time and nourishment to develop along leaderful dimensions. Figure 3.3 displays continua of leaderful team development along five such dimensions:

1. The degree of discretion in how team members interpret and transact the skills inherent in their job

FIGURE **3.3**

The Continua of Leaderful Team Development

Discretion	Low Discretion	←——————→	High Discretion
Autonomy	Seeks Permission	←——————→	Autonomous
Empowerment	Over Own Tasks Only	←——————→	Beyond the Job
Motivation	Calculative	←——————→	Intrinsic
Culture	Control-Oriented	←——————→	Trust-Oriented

2. The autonomy they exhibit toward the key decisions in their work
3. The empowerment they may feel toward shaping actions and decisions beyond their own sphere of work
4. The extent to which their motivation is intrinsic suggesting genuine care about their job, team, and organization
5. The degree to which they would characterize their work culture as trust-oriented rather than control-oriented

The right endpoint of each of the continua specifies the more leaderful properties.

....

ACTIVITY 3.5

Mapping the Continuum of Leaderful Team Development

The steps in this activity focus on the team rather than on individual team members and can be used on multiple occasions to assess the team's development.

STEP 1: Display the continua of Figure 3.3 to all team members. Be sure to explain the meanings of these continua. Each places a mark where he or she feels the team currently resides along each of the five continua.

STEP 2: Members share their results and explain why they placed the mark where they did.

STEP 3: Try to arrive at a team consensus on where they feel the team currently resides on the five continua.

STEP 4: Discuss as a team how its processes and interactions may need to change to move the current state to the right (on each continuum).

STEP 5: Repeat this activity at subsequent points in the team's life to determine if there is growth in the direction of more leaderful practice.

....

Improving My Team

Perhaps the most apt use of team facilitation is to improve the functioning of one's own team. Facilitation skills are often used to focus on immediate issues that affect the team in the here-and-now, but team effectiveness cannot be achieved if process facilitation occurs only when problems arise. Just as musical groups and sports teams need to rehearse and practice, work teams need to practice how to become more effective in both their task and maintenance roles.

···

ACTIVITY 3.6

Team Reflective Practice for Self-Renewal

This activity uses reflective practice skills to improve any team that may be at a point of equilibrium but that may nevertheless benefit from critical self-renewal.

STEP 1: Take some private moments to allow members of the team to think of an issue that they believe is impeding the team's performance.

STEP 2: When ready, some of the members describe what they have thought about and explain what they see as the possible impact on the team.

STEP 3: Team members focus on one of the issues and ask other members to react to what has been observed about the team and how they see it.

STEP 4: Another team member is asked to clarify and summarize what the team has heard.

STEP 5: In your role as facilitator, you, or any other facilitating member, asks the team as a whole whether the issue that has been raised is one worth tackling right now. If not, it should be tabled for another time, but members should commit to having a dialogue about the issue at a definitive point. If the team is able to work on the issue right now, members should proceed to suggest ways to manage the issue that they have been discussing.

···

....

CASE STUDY

Facilitating a Team During Its Growing Pains

Joe Raelin

I had the pleasure of facilitating a learning team in conjunction with an action learning intervention within a large utility company. The team was concurrently a project team assigned to carry out a critical strategic assignment provided by a sponsor who was also a top manager within the corporate hierarchy. There were three other learning teams working at the same time, and the overall program had been in existence for several years prior to the current cohort. The project that this team was working on had to do with the need to improve the perception that local municipalities had of the work of this utility's distribution function—namely, the laying of pipes and wires.

There were a number of instances, especially in the early going when, as the learning team facilitator, I had to implement some of the facilitation guidelines discussed in Activity 3.1, "Learning to Facilitate." This case demonstrates the use of three of these specific guidelines and the impact they had.

1. *Encourage members to speak freely.* The team appeared to be a "doer" team, wanting to jump right into their project and solve the problem. For example, most of the members wanted to develop a survey right away to distribute to city and town public officials regarding service issues. One of the members (we'll call him Tom), however, kept challenging what he considered to be some untested assumptions regarding their "charge" from the sponsor. On three occasions, his request to review an underlying assumption was ignored by the group.

    As the team's facilitator, I wanted to support Tom because of the value our action learning program was placing on challenging assumptions as a way to promote more open dialogue. At the same time, I did not want to berate the other members who were exhibiting some spontaneous energy to attack the problem presented to the team by their sponsor. Another important consideration was that the members had received some individual feedback on their learning styles, and the only member of the team who was high on the "reflective" style was this challenger, Tom.

    So, after his third attempt to persuade the group to reconsider its approach to launch a survey, I said the following:

    "Tom, I can see that you honestly object to the approach being considered here, and I appreciate your willingness to take an alternative point of view. I can also appreciate, as others have pointed out, that the team seems to have picked up some momentum in launching this survey. So, I'm wondering if we can just give you some bounded time to explain in a bit more detail what your objections are to the survey as currently constructed?"

After this intervention, a couple of members voiced their consent to have Tom expound in more depth. Further, Tom seemed to develop a little more confidence to try to explain his objections. He disclosed his views, albeit in a lumbering style, in some detail. It turns out that one of his objections was the team's avoidance of surveying regular customers, who, after all, were at the same time citizens of their communities. A number of the members picked up on this objection and began to think of ways to incorporate a sample of the citizenry rather than direct the survey to only representative officials.

After a flurry of activity on a survey redesign, I asked the group if they'd like to debrief the interaction following Tom's initial dissent. A number of members spoke up that indeed they were guilty of plunging ahead too quickly, almost frenetically, and needed to slow down. They recognized the value of having Tom, the "reflector," help them incorporate some elements of the survey that would otherwise have constituted some serious omissions. One of the members even thanked Tom for "sticking to his guns," and asked him to keep them honest henceforth.

2. *Don't suppress conflict; recognize and manage it.* Still at a relatively early point in the team's development, a conflict arose about the lack of speed with which the team was accomplishing its mission. Some of the members were becoming anxious when they compared the team's relative rate of progress to that of the other teams, which, at a full community session, had given promising status reports. My own view at the time was that we were laying some important groundwork and were not truly "behind" the other teams, although it may have appeared to be so. In one instance, two of the members directed a challenge to me directly by asking if they could switch groups to a project that was more interesting but also more likely to be successfully implemented. My immediate reaction was to become defensive, since, after all, as the facilitator I took some responsibility for their progress, including their commitment to the team. Knowing that a defensive reaction would not have been helpful, I swallowed my initial impulse and decided instead to make a statement that, though a risk, would bring both the anxiety of the team and the likely conflict that stemmed from it out into the open.

My response was, "It looks like you both feel that we're falling behind but also that, if we are, it is likely to be my fault. Can we explore these two contentions as assumptions?"

What I was trying to do was to legitimate the challenges to my own facilitation but also to model an exploration of them in a way that recognized the conflict but gave it a chance to be addressed openly. Initially, the team decided to look at each of the challenges in turn. A few of the members subsequently felt a need to come to my immediate defense, with one even saying that we should "lay off Joe" and consider our own inadequacies as a team. I made another intervention at this point to say that we don't have to focus on me personally right now. Let's test the assumption, first, that we're falling behind and then we can explore our views about the role of facilitation in learning teams.

The team then earnestly got into the issue of our pace of development. Members discussed a range of issues, from the perspective of project planning to a consideration of the socioemotional foundation needed to develop the team. Before we knew it, an hour had passed and we still hadn't gotten to the issue of my facilitation style. Some members offered their views on this issue, but we had to table further discussion until the next meeting when it, too, consumed our attention, in this case for approximately 45 minutes. The consensus was that as the facilitator I should not be responsible for the output of the group, but that if I had strong opinions about our performance, I might offer my feedback more spontaneously. I agreed to do so, but such feedback became less needed as the group matured in its evolution.

3. *Model inquiry.* During one of the next meetings, two team members were curiously silent during nearly an entire morning discussion about plans for composing a citizen's survey. In the afternoon learning team meeting, one of the members pointed out that she hadn't heard from these two members and wanted to know what was on their minds. I then asked the team if we could use this instance as an opportunity for some personal inquiry. They agreed and so I suggested that we first formulate a few questions that we'd like to ask, not only these members, but of each other. First, we'd ask each person if he or she would be willing to explore his or her feelings about our progress so far as a project team. Anyone could opt out of this kind of conversation at any point. We would then ask that speaker to proceed and give any illustrations to exemplify his or her points. After finishing, someone might attempt to summarize the points to be sure that everyone in the team understood the speaker. Thereafter, others would come forward to offer their views and interpretations of what the speaker said. This would lead to a fuller conversation, keeping the focus on the speaker's ideas and concerns.

We proceeded with this inquiry and were able to give three members a chance to speak, including the two "quiet" members. It turned out that each of the two had a completely different reason for his and her silence.

One of the members had been completely frustrated by the tangents that had come into play during the morning discussion and couldn't believe the team didn't immediately adopt a tried-and-true approach that he and others he knew had always used. He was simply impatient. However, the exchange led to his consideration of others' points of view. He also admitted that in his managerial capacity he was nearly always used to having things go his way, but he was opening up to the idea of working through a multitude of perspectives. The other quiet member admitted that as a fresh young supervisor, she didn't feel that she could offer a credible argument on behalf of any of the alternatives, especially with some of the experienced and talented engineers in the room. Most of the members reacted in an encouraging manner to this team member, saying that her experience from being in the field would be invaluable and that she should not at all feel a need to restrict her input in this way. We were all equal when it came to our contributions to this project. The team concluded this activity with many expressing relief that we had let some fresh air into the room and that no one should ever feel held back.

These three interventions, in my view, each contributed to constructive leaderful development for this team. In the first, the team developed a greater appreciation of the value of dissent, allowing members to be freer in contributing their full leadership to the team. In the second, the team recognized the value of bringing conflict out into the open, which led to the incorporation of a number of collaborative processes, such as recognizing anxiety, raising assumptions, advocating firmly, querying others, and facilitating change. The third modeled an inquiry process that sought to bring the "undiscussables" out into the open in a way that promoted fuller participation by all team members.

Chapter Four

Organization-Level Change

A T THE ORGANIZATIONAL OR INSTITUTIONAL LEVEL OF CHANGE, learners may aspire to have leaderful practices systemically or informally diffused throughout the organization and, in some cases, across the organization into other stakeholder entities. When accomplished, managers and workers should feel comfortable challenging existing mindsets and entering into a dialogue across their own subcultural boundaries. However, a special challenge is creating a culture of learning in which it's acceptable to dialogue openly about such undiscussable topics as forbidden themes, defensive routines, conflicts of interest, or power relations. The change agent most appropriate at this level is the organizational development (OD) consultant who is trained to encourage the emergence of a leaderful culture that values learning and democratic participation.

The OD consultant, often an external change agent, attempts to improve organizations by applying knowledge from the behavioral sciences to help their members enhance their collaborative processes. As change agents, OD consultants attempt to mold structures and systems that tolerate dissent and encourage open communication. In particular, they try to make sure that people and teams have access to information, power and freedom, and plentiful learning opportunities. In that way, everyone in the organization is involved in co-creating the entity. OD change requires far more than mere "support from the top." Support from the top does not go deep enough; unless sustained throughout the organization, any change or transformation won't hold. People will keep quiet about what they know or use double-talk because of past experiences that may have led to fear or blame. They need to see that any change has been institutionalized as an organizational norm.

OD consultants as change agents are aware how cultural artifacts of the organization, whether longstanding stories about cult figures, current examples of new behavior, or rewards that reinforce collaboration can powerfully shape cultural norms. As an example, consider an oft-told story about "the millwright," a saga cherished at the office furnisher maker Herman Miller. The story, reported in Max De Pree's *Leadership Is an Art*,[14] is used to illustrate Herman Miller's value of honoring the integrity of the individual and, in particular, the diversity of people's gifts, talents, and skills. D. J. De Pree, the founder of the company, would visit the family of any key employee who passed away. He would go to the family's house and spend time in the living room, typically in awkward conversation. One day the millwright died, and De Pree went to the home of his widow. She asked D. J. if she could read some poetry aloud. He agreed, so she read several pieces of beautiful poetry. When she finished, the young De Pree commented on how poignant the poetry was and asked who wrote it. She replied that her husband, the millwright, was the poet. D. J. always wondered, as do many others at Herman Miller, whether this man was a poet who did millwright's work or whether he was a millwright who happened to write poetry.

The seven activities in this chapter are designed to help you, as a veteran or prospective OD consultant, work effectively with learners and also with organizational sponsors to produce more collaborative and more reflective exchanges leading to cultures receptive to leaderful practices.

The first activity, **Brokering Leaderful Change**, identifies the elements of a social change process, names the critical roles occupied by the change agent as well as by the key stakeholders to the change, and anticipates the landmines of change.

The second activity, **Closing the Gap Between Espoused and Enacted Values**, highlights the importance of culture as a gateway into the values that guide organizational behavior and helps learners identify the artifacts of their organization's culture, whether the values they represent are espoused or enacted, and how to transition into an enacted leaderful culture.

The third activity, **Acting on Our Leaderful Values**, encourages learners to assess their performance on some of the most critical values

---

[14] M. De Pree, *Leadership Is an Art* (New York: Doubleday, 1989).

of leaderful practice and how any named barriers to their practice can be overcome.

The fourth activity, **Picturing the Self and Organization**, captures and promotes reflection on the role and responsibility of the learner relative to an organization to which he or she is affiliated, and which is about to experience change.

The fifth activity, **Demonstrating Organizational Commitment**, introduces the Organizational Commitment Survey to provide the opportunity for learners to assess their commitment and citizenship behavior on behalf of their organization and to dialogue about differences and patterns across their survey scores.

The sixth activity, **Meaning-Making Skills**, introduces the concept and practice of meaning making by having learners practice a set of meaning-making skills and determine whether these can bring coherence to an unclear or uncertain situation.

The seventh activity, **Assessment of Worker Participation**, assesses the level of worker participation in the organization and, as a basis for leaderful practice, determines whether steps can be taken to involve workers in a range of organizational decisions and outcomes.

Leaderful Change

The leaderful change agent is not the visionary who pulls the organization to where he or she wants it to go. Instead, as servants of the organization, leaderful change agents mobilize the members of the organization to change in the direction that they wish to go. They work at creating a psychologically safe environment that encourages everyone to contribute to remake the organization into as compassionate and uplifting a social system as it can be.

Leaderful practice relies on two principles underlying learners' commitment to collaborative action. First, it knows that when people participate in designing a change that they see as desirable, their self-identity becomes tied to the successful implementation of the change. Hence, they become intrinsically motivated not only to see the change implemented but implemented successfully. Second, when individuals participate in a change effort, they typically structure the change to be ultimately desirable to them. So by involving people in change, leaderful agents by their very behavior and instincts overcome a good part of the natural resistance that most people have toward change itself.

Activity 4.1, presented in multiple parts, is designed to help relatively experienced OD consultants consider change agency from a leaderful perspective.

....

ACTIVITY 4.1

Brokering Leaderful Change

OD consultants by definition do not transact change on their own; rather, they are brokers of change working with others involved in the change process, including those who are directly affected by the change. Activity 4.1, then, is best accomplished with your colleagues or with the change team involved in particular interventions.

STEP 1: Following are the stages in a social change model derived by the author. As you view each stage, you are encouraged to consider the listed queries through dialogue with your colleagues and clients.

1. Challenge the old policy with valid information.
   - Do we have access to concrete data that are disconfirming the present state of affairs?
   - What would happen if we were to keep our current state?
   - What from our old policy can be conserved?
2. Allow mourning.
   - What interests have been served by the old policy that might have to be given up?
   - Who is being negatively affected? Can they be compensated?
   - What are we losing?
   - What resources are available to help us overcome any loss?
3. Co-create the new policy.
   - Who is sponsoring this change and why?
   - What will we become after the change?
   - Do people understand what is happening to them and why?
   - Who has been overlooked in mounting the change?
4. Provide opportunities for new learning.

- What of a technical nature needs to be learned so that we can fully understand any new subject matter?
- How should any knowledge acquisition be accomplished?
- What of an administrative nature needs to be learned to manage the change?
- Are structures in place to manage the process?
- Are individuals prepared for handling some of the emotional undercurrents?

5. Institutionalize the new policy.
   - Are there models, examples, or data to cite to demonstrate effectiveness?
   - Is the reward structure compatible with the new change?
   - What percentage of the affected population is truly involved?
   - Are we prepared to report the results of the change and compare them to the prior policy?
   - Are we ready to make adjustments based upon our ongoing assessments?

STEP 2: The next step is to determine the multiple roles that are played out in any change scenario. There are roles to be considered by the change agent; then there are roles assumed by the plethora of stakeholders with whom the change team needs to interact.

Consider the following eight roles based on the work of Gordon and Ronald Lippitt[15] that could be adopted by the OD consultant. Notice that they are arrayed on the basis of the activeness of the intervention, from the most active to the most passive.

1. Advocate
2. Information provider
3. Instructor/trainer
4. Joint problem solver
5. Linker
6. Fact finder
7. Process counselor
8. Observer

---

[15] G. Lippitt and R. Lippitt, *The Consulting Process in Action*, 2nd ed. (San Diego, CA: University Associates, 1986).

In this step, try to hone in on one of these eight roles as most appropriate for the phase of the change that you are currently considering. As you contemplate which role would be most appropriate, keep in mind a number of considerations:

• The nature of your relationship to the client
• Expectations for the nature and scope of the change
• Goals of the intervention
• Preferences on the part of the client
• Preferences on your part as the consultant
• The culture of the entity and the parties involved

Now consider the roles that various stakeholders might play or need to play in the interventions that are being contemplated for a change scenario. The task of identifying stakeholders will be more formally introduced in chapter 5, but for purposes of this activity, consider stakeholders to be important individuals or constituencies whose involvement is important to the success of the venture. Identifying these stakeholders and their respective roles should be completed with your colleagues and change team.

Your change team will need to break up your contemplated change scenario into a series of component interventions or parts. For example, you may wish to entertain the format called "Planned Change" and include such steps as establishing a relationship, conducting the diagnosis, planning for action, taking action, evaluating (and replanning, if necessary). Your team might prefer instead to break the change scenario down by content areas or processes (develop a history, consult best practices, form a design team, conduct a survey, feed back results, evaluate responses, map an implementation plan) or by location.

To complete this last step, your team is invited to fill in the Actor Responsibility Matrix in Figure 4.1 by assigning each stakeholder a role designation for each element of the intervention. Note that some stakeholders may hold more than one role.

STEP 3: Having identified the roles occupied by key stakeholders to the change, obtain a sense about the overall reception to the prospective change by everyone potentially affected within your organization. A model known as the "Diffusion of Innovations," originally conceived by Everett M. Rogers,[16] can be helpful in mapping how people generally respond to proposed change interventions. These responses are proposed to follow a reasonably predictable

---

[16] E. M. Rogers, *Diffusion of Innovations*, 5th ed. (New York: Free Press, 2003).

FIGURE **4.1**

Actor Responsibility Matrix

Instructions: Please fill in the matrix headings, and then write in the cells the letter corresponding to the following roles.

Advocate (A): Champion of the change but often lacking the power to sanction it; often someone in middle management who strongly supports the effort and who can build commitment and enthusiasm but who lacks sufficient resources or authority

Sponsor (S): Usually an individual in upper management who can mobilize resources to effect a change because of his or her authority and budgetary powers

Change agent (C) The individual(s) who are on the ground and who wish to prove the concept and make things happen; could be the OD consultant and his or her team

Target (T): The individual or group directly affected by the intervention whose involvement will be critical in the operation and evaluation of the change

Networkers (N): People whose opinions matter because they link with other key stakeholders and can either sell or resist the change efforts

Resistors1 (R_1): The open resistors who oppose the effort but are willing to give their reasons why the change should be legitimately opposed

Resistors2 (R_2): The quiet resistors who are opposed to the effort but are unwilling to disclose their reasons either because they are timid or because they believe their cause is better advanced through subterfuge

Intervention/Actor	Sara: Top manager	Thomas: R&D director	[List others]		
Establish a diagnosis	S, R_1	A			
Plan the intervention	S	A			
[List additional tasks]					

pattern comparable to a bell curve. There will be shifts in the so-called adopter population depending upon the intervention in question, but to begin the analysis, consider the five categories of adopters:

1. The *innovators*, comprising only 2.5 percent of the adopter population, are courageous and foresighted individuals interested in trying out the new idea or practice.

2. The *early adopters*, constituting the next 13.5 percent, tend to be respected opinion leaders who, though careful, are encouraging of new ideas and practices.

3. The *early majority*, some 34 percent of adopters, are thoughtful individuals who tend to be cautious but are more accepting of change than the average population.

4. The *late majority*, containing also 34 percent, are skeptical and will use new ideas or practices only when the majority is on board.

5. The *laggards*, consisting of the last 16 percent, are traditionalists who are set in their ways, thereupon suspicious of new ideas and practices, and willing to accept them only if they have become mainstream.

Once having distributed the affected population across these initial categories, invite the change team to consider a number of probing questions that make use of the data:

- If you were to consider other related interventions in the domain of the prospective change, would people fall into and out of the categories? Would the percentages shift?

- Does it make sense to work with all categories equally, or should you focus your efforts on those most supportive or potentially supportive?

- Are there ways you might communicate the change that could cause a shift in the categories? What if you proposed that the change be more or less "trialable," that is, to be considered experimental over a bounded period of time?

- Are there other considerations that might cause shifts in the suggested adopter populations, such as communication of benefits, costs, risks, or compatibility with existing standards or values?

- In your organization and for the change in question, what percentage of the population needs to adopt it for it to take effect?

STEP 4: In this last step, the OD consultant has a final chance to anticipate some of the resistance that especially late adopters are likely to mount against any kind of leaderful change, as in a classic vignette referred to here as "The Landmines of Change."

The Landmines of Change

A formerly autocratic manager turns over a new leaf and professes to become more democratic. He decides to delegate more responsibility to one of his workers. Naturally, the worker, having lived under the autocratic thumb of this boss for many years, mistrusts the manager's motives. In the past, whenever any subordinates took some initiative on a project and appeared to fail, the boss would punish them in some way, such as by taking away the assignment. So, the worker takes a wait-and-see attitude, expecting that, in due course, the boss will tell her what to do.

Meanwhile, the boss perceives this worker's hesitation as a sign of dependency. He figures that he was right all along, that this individual is lazy and can't be trusted to assume responsibility. The boss takes back the project and vows never to take this kind of risk again. The worker, meanwhile, feels vindicated that her view of the boss was correct, and she vows, in turn, to never accept new levels of responsibility if ever asked to again.

This vignette highlights a number of *landmines*—or latent barriers—in the path of leaderful change that you and your colleagues should review prior to undertaking the relevant change effort. Consider, then, the following landmines and the queries attached to them:

The "Wisdom" of the Status Quo

- Why has the current situation been allowed to persist without change up to this point?
- Who is being protected or privileged by the status quo?

Lack of Patience

- How can we overlook some of the expected errors that might occur when people not normally empowered take the reins?
- Do we sincerely trust those at lower levels, or even at our own level, to manage operations and processes that we may have formerly overseen?

Low Readiness for Change

- What is the stage of readiness of the system in question? For example, are people truly interested in taking responsibility?

- What resources have been made available to prepare people for the change?

Attempt to Apply "Fix-It" Techniques

- Has the effort considered any side effects of the change as well as its long-term implications?
- Has the effort taken into consideration people's individual agendas, including their feelings and values, on the issue in question?

Belief That We Can Decree Change

- Are people truly committed to the change, both in its process and its anticipated outcomes?
- As the change agent, are you willing to step outside of the center and let others shape the process?

Organizational Culture

An important method for assessing the potential to engage in leaderful change at the organizational level is to analyze the organization's culture. *Culture* in this context is often defined as the set of shared, taken-for-granted, often implicit, assumptions that shape behavior. It is also thought to have significant effects on such organizational conditions as strategy, employee satisfaction, and performance. In fact, research studies have demonstrated a link between culture and employee attitudes and behavior and have suggested, furthermore, that when there is congruence between the individual's and the organization's values, the effect on the organization in terms of employee commitment and satisfaction is quite positive. The reason for culture's impact is that it is thought to give members of any system a sense of belongingness and identity. Although any organization's culture can be broken down by its various subcultures, there are often close parallels, especially when the systemwide culture is dominant.

An organization's culture can be manifested through a number of observable vehicles, such as the way the organization organizes its office structure or space, any mission statements, its jargon or language, stories and myths that are transmitted from generation to generation, how people talk to one another, or even manner of dress.

These so-called artifacts can be studied to reveal the organization's values—those beliefs that can serve as a guide to the way people should act in the organization. When using culture as a starting point for useful OD interventions in an organization, one must know whether there is consistency between the values that are espoused by the organization and those that are enacted, as well as how to enact those values that are democratic in nature.

....

ACTIVITY 4.2

Closing the Gap Between Espoused and Enacted Values

Espoused values are those that the organization claims to follow, whereas its *enacted values* are those that define how the members of the organization or its units truly act. If there is consistency across these values, there should be less confusion in orchestrating leaderful change, because any meaningful gap between the organization's affirmed values and actual behavior will be minimal, promoting a degree of authenticity. In most organizations and units, however, we find that gaps are ever present. Further, if leaderful change is to occur at the organizational level, it not only has to be espoused but also enacted by people in the organization (including those in power). This activity consists of a number of steps, ending with the OD consultant working with a change team to implement a leaderful culture at the enacted level.

STEP 1: Determine the current culture's enacted values.
Assemble the key stakeholders to any prospective change and work through a brainstorming procedure to list the artifacts and experiences that point to the organization's culture or the unit's subculture, depending upon the level in which you are concentrating.
Let the stakeholders give examples of the following:

- Important stories and myths
- Jargon and language
- Physical organization of space
- Work arrangements
- Manner of addressing one another
- Mission statements and other published lists
- Ceremonies, rituals, and rewards

- Manner of dress

Besides artifacts, the culture of the organization or subunit can be inferred from what people do as well as from tacit experiences and processes, such as decision making, which may be less easily recordable or observable. In these instances, ask the team to describe some of the important processes, experiences, and identities that may reveal the organization's enacted values. Some questions to consider include:

- Who seems to get the benefits and perks in this organization and why?
- Who seems to get in trouble in this organization and why?
- Which roles are deemed most valuable? Which are considered least valuable?
- Is there an orientation (for example, based on expenditures, risk, functionality) that seems to prevail whenever important decisions are made?
- What stands out to newcomers to this organization?

Conclude this step by listing the enacted values that characterize the organization's culture:

- [example] That the important decisions get made at the top and are transmitted down the chain of command.
- [example] That people with an accounting orientation seem to flourish in our company.
- [continue with your own examples]

Please note that you could also choose to do this brainstorming in smaller groups—perhaps by unit or at random—and then share the results with a larger group.

STEP 2: Uncover the current culture's espoused values.
Brainstorm with the team the espoused values of the organization or unit. The espoused values are those that are presented and described in both the internal and external media or are articulated by verbal and written messages, usually from the organization's authorities.

STEP 3: Identify the gap between the enacted and espoused values.
If the lists of values produced in Steps 1 and 2 are compatible, you can skip this step, but you will likely find such compatibility to be rare. So, assuming there are differences across these two lists, engage the group in a discussion

about the implications of the gap between the enacted and espoused values. Are there beneficiaries of the gap? Would some people gain or lose out if the gap were to be filled? What are the short-term and long-term limitations (and possible benefits) from having an inconsistency between the enacted and espoused values?

STEP 4: Define the desired espoused culture.

Based on the lists and discussions held so far, engage in a dialogue about the proposed changes that the team would recommend in order for the culture to be more leaderful. The assumption here is that leaderful practice represents a set of espoused values that are endorsed by the group—that is, that the organization be more concurrent and collective in its leadership, more collaborative, and more compassionate. What values would the organization or unit need to adopt? How would day-to-day behavior need to change? What artifacts would represent the desired culture; for example, the look and feel of the place? Who would have to change in his or her manner of dealing with others? Which practices would need to be emphasized? Which deemphasized?

STEP 5: Enact the desired culture.

End the dialogue by listing and discussing a set of implementation steps—the actions (and deliverables) that need to be taken to operationalize any of the leaderful changes specified in Step 4. This requires a transformation from the existing enacted values to the desired espoused values. Would there have to be a series of meetings or colloquia to voice some of the proposed changes? How else would they be communicated and discussed? Would the changes require new learning, and if so, how would the new learning be acquired? Since the original enacted values provided benefits to some individuals, how would these individuals be approached about changes that might disturb their current disposition? What new forms of information would need to be provided? Would there need to be a shift in people's rights and responsibilities? How would the new values be monitored over time to determine if the new culture "is sticking"?

Leaderful Values

Activity 4.2 brought out the criticality of values in diagnosing and understanding an organization's culture. As we have seen, values are not necessarily articulated, but they underlie our motives for acting, especially when we make important decisions. Most people operate out of their values. In leaderful practice, the inherent values are democratic in character because acting leaderfully signifies behavior performed in conjunction with the members of one's organization or organizational unit. Going back to a fundamental tenet of humanism, one is not inclined to make decisions without including people who are affected by that decision.

Values affect how people in the organization approach their jobs and how they may refer to such criteria as success or effectiveness. Values may also be applied to either the processes or the outcomes of relationships. In the first instance, we may use ethical criteria to determine whether we treat one another well or with respect. In the second instance, we become concerned with the effects of our actions on the multiple stakeholders with whom we interact. We may have met our economic goals as an organization, for example, but may have done so without paying sufficient attention to the people with whom we have come into contact, and have thus lost their confidence.

....

ACTIVITY 4.3

Acting on Our Leaderful Values

This is a concise activity that reviews some of the values that learners may wish to explicitly recognize and practice during any intervention or project entailing OD change.

STEP 1: Learners first reflect on a list of leaderful values and indicate the degree to which they and other colleagues involved in a specific intervention or change scenario practice them. Use Figure 4.2 to complete this step.

STEP 2: If you or colleagues have not been able to practice some of these important values, then by yourself and in conjunction with your colleagues try to discern the barriers that are getting in the way along five, now familiar, dimensions:

   a. *Personal* [example: I don't have enough courage or I'm fearful of the consequences]

   b. *Interpersonal* [example: We lack trust or we are choosing to be self-protective]

   c. *Team* [example: Our norms don't make room for full participation by everyone or we are too concerned about completing the task]

FIGURE **4.2**

The Practice of Leaderful Values

Instructions: In the second and fourth columns, use the following rating scale to complete your ratings: 5—To a great extent; 4—To a moderate extent; 3—To a slight extent; 2—Rarely; 1—Not at all.

Leaderful Values	To what extent do you practice them	Evidence to substanti-ate your rating	To what ex-tent do your colleagues practice them	Evidence to substanti-ate your rating
Humility—No person has inherent superiority over others				
Respect—My contribution is dependent upon others				
Diversity—Other cultures and viewpoints are honored				
Access—People have the data and resources that they need				
Localness—Those who do the work closest to the problem are empowered				
De-leveling—Planning is consolidated with doing				
Job Identity—The whole job is seen through to the end				

    d. *Organization* [example: The culture of our organization is conformist or these values are merely espoused but not practiced]

    e. *Network* [example: There are important stakeholders whose voices have not been heard or have been stifled]

STEP 3: Individually and then with your partners, discuss how you might overcome the most critical barriers.

The Self Within the Organization

From Activities 4.2 and 4.3, we can see that our values significantly shape our leadership practices because they inform the way we handle ourselves when interacting with others. Further, it is certainly easier to engage productively with others when our values coincide largely with those consistently espoused and enacted within the organization and its units. As part of preparing for change, OD consultants need to determine whether their individual clients (and perhaps they themselves) perceive their roles and responsibilities to their organizations to be intimately connected to and appreciated by the organization. If so, there will be both inclusion and connectedness between the self and the organization; if not, they may feel excluded and disconnected, in which case they may choose to sit on the sidelines during any change event.

....

ACTIVITY 4.4

Picturing the Self and Organization

This activity, suggested by my colleague Michael Butler-Burns, invites learners to pictorially depict their view of their organization and their role in it. Initially, they characterize the condition of their organization or organizational unit and subsequently follow up with a depiction of themselves in relation to the organization.

STEP 1: Assemble a group of learners who are committed to a search for an understanding about their role in relation to an organization facing change. Explain that this will be a personal exercise, involving disclosures that may be shared with trusted others, and is preparatory to organizational change.

STEP 2: Each learner draws a picture (it could be an image or shape) that depicts the organization or organizational unit at this time, prior to any change. The decision whether to draw one's organization or unit is important and should be based on whichever system will afford the higher degree of learning. In conjunction with this step, the assembled learners may be invited to engage with you either individually or in the group about the value of drawing an image to represent an organization. You can point out that by resorting to images or shapes, we are not beholden to theoretical constructs but rather can let our minds flow in reproducing an image or images that can capture our perception about how things "get done around here." There is no need for pure accuracy, since we are interested in people's perceptions.

STEP 3: The learners include themselves in the picture, using whatever image or shape comes to mind. You can clarify that you are interested in their attempting to capture their relationship to the organizational world, thinking, for example, of any roles and responsibilities that they assume. You might repeat that this image would characterize where they are right now in relation to the current organization or unit. Learners may ask whether they need to put themselves directly within the prior image, in which case you might suggest that such a positioning would be left completely to their own discretion. They need to capture the relationship between themselves and the organization however they truly see it.

STEP 4: The learners prepare a separate image, but like the one completed in Step 3, it contains both the organization and themselves in relation to one another. However, in this step, they depict how the organization might become after an expected or imagined change and how the learner would be depicted in relationship to the organization under this changed condition. In most cases, the picture captured in the prior steps will look quite a bit different from the picture drawn here.

STEP 5: This step is for feedback and reflection on each of the two pictures. It is preferable to have learners work on one picture at a time and compare them afterward. By launching into a comparison first, they may miss some important revelations available in their initial drawings. Although you can make yourself available to each learner as a coach, it might be beneficial for the learners to seek out a small team of their colleagues, perhaps those already assembled for the activity, and to begin the sharing process as peer mentors to one another.
Here are some of the questions that might be posed during this last step:

Picture of the Organization Now

- What does your image say about the state of the organization or unit as it currently stands?
- What specific features would you like to point out that may not be obvious to others?
- Why did you depict yourself in relation to the organization in the way that you did?

- What does your self-depiction say about your current involvement in your organization and about your opportunity to steward any form of change?
- How would you draw the comparison between your values and those of your organization or unit?

Picture of the Changed Organization

- What does the organization look like in the changed condition? Is it more favorable than in its current state?
- Are you engaged in the changed condition? In what capacity?
- What is the nature of the change that would lead to the image you have crafted?

Differences Between the Two Pictures

- How would you characterize the difference between the first and second pictures?
- If your role and responsibilities are different, what are the differences and what has or would lead to their being so?
- What do the picture changes say about you and your values?

Organizational Commitment

People develop commitment and loyalty to an organization for a host of reasons. Some might choose to remain part of an organization (or unit) because they perceive no other options, because their social network is present, or because "significant others" expect them to stay. However, the form of commitment thought to be most related to leaderful practice, both as a cause as well as an outcome, is *affective commitment*, or emotional commitment to remain with an organization because of what it stands for. When one has affective commitment, one is willing to help the organization achieve its goals. In some instances, committed employees are willing to contribute to an organization by engaging in organizational citizenship behavior, that is, by taking actions that, though not recognized by the formal reward system, are performed anyway to help the organization.

....

ACTIVITY 4.5

Demonstrating Organizational Commitment

In this activity, learners who might also be key policymakers or stakeholders in the organization (or unit) are assembled to register their personal feelings of commitment to the organization. The group assembled should contain individuals who are willing to openly discuss their feelings of organizational commitment based on the results of an organizational commitment survey.

STEP 1: Individual members of the group assembled first fill out the Organizational Commitment Survey in Figure 4.3. They can fill out the survey prior to attending or at the time of a meeting to discuss the results, but they should in either instance be informed about the principal and potential value of organizational commitment as well as the underlying concept of organizational citizenship behavior.

STEP 2: The learners in the assembled group sum the totals in each of the five columns. Based on an idea from John Newstrom and Keith Davis,[17] they score their organizational commitment survey by using the following formula (note that the letters correspond to the total scores for each of the five ratings):

$$\text{Organizational Commitment (OC) Index} = \frac{2a + b - d - 2e}{40}$$

Convert the OC Index into a decimal. It is possible to score in negative figures. The highest or perfect score would be a 1.0.

STEP 3: The learners next furnish you with their scores. Compile these by preparing a frequency distribution displaying the range of individual total scores. Share the results. Next, with everyone present and using a show of hands, write down the frequencies for each item, going from the first to the twentieth behavior. Everyone should examine the total index score data as well as these item-by-item results and privately write in their journals what these scores suggest to them.

STEP 4: Once everyone has reflected on the scoring patterns, initiate a dialogue in which learners consider the following questions (on page 110):

---

[17] J. Newstrom and K. Davis, *Organizational Behavior: Readings and Exercises*, 8th ed. (New York: McGraw-Hill, 1989), p. 547.

FIGURE **4.3**

Organizational Commitment Survey*

Instructions: Please fill out this survey by checking one of five agreement ratings attached to each listed behavior in relation to your organization.

Behaviors	My rating (check one)				
	Agree a Lot (a)	Agree Some- what (b)	Neutral (c)	Dis- agree Some- what (d)	Dis- agree a Lot (e)
Do you:					
1. Represent the organization favorably to outsiders?	___	___	___	___	___
2. Offer ideas to help improve the functioning of the organization?	___	___	___	___	___
3. Reliably report instances of others breaking our ethical code?	___	___	___	___	___
4. Respect any confidences associated with your position?	___	___	___	___	___
5. Go out of your way to defend the organization against external threats?	___	___	___	___	___
6. Offer extra time to help the organization even when not required?	___	___	___	___	___
7. Help orient newcomers to the organization?	___	___	___	___	___
8. Help others who have heavy workloads?	___	___	___	___	___
9. Voluntarily attend functions to further the organization's image?	___	___	___	___	___
10. Defend the organization when others criticize it?	___	___	___	___	___
11. Take action to protect the organization from potential problems?	___	___	___	___	___

(Continued on next page)

FIGURE **4.3** *(Continued)*

Behaviors	My rating (check one)				
	Agree a Lot (a)	Agree Somewhat (b)	Neutral (c)	Disagree Somewhat (d)	Disagree a Lot (e)
12. Stay active in outside groups or clubs that promote the organization's general interests?	_____	_____	_____	_____	_____
13. Hold work goals above personal nonwork goals?	_____	_____	_____	_____	_____
14. Monitor and limit the amount of personal time taken at work?	_____	_____	_____	_____	_____
15. Keep up to date about the organization's products or services?	_____	_____	_____	_____	_____
16. Work at home to finish a job if necessary?	_____	_____	_____	_____	_____
17. Assume extra duties and responsibilities to help the organization?	_____	_____	_____	_____	_____
18. Volunteer for committee work?	_____	_____	_____	_____	_____
19. Keep informed about matters that might benefit the organization?	_____	_____	_____	_____	_____
20. Offer a minority opinion if it will help the organization's agenda?	_____	_____	_____	_____	_____
Totals:	_____	_____	_____	_____	_____

* Adapted from scales in the domain of organizational citizenship behavior (OCB), in particular: K. Lee and N. J. Allen, "Organizational Citizenship Behavior and Workplace Deviance: The Role of Affect and Cognitions," *Journal of Applied Psychology*, 87, pp. 131–142, 2002; J. Newstrom and K. Davis, *Organizational Behavior: Readings and Exercises*, 8th ed. (New York: McGraw-Hill, 1989), pp. 548–549; C. A. Smith, D. W. Organ, and J. P. Near, "Organizational Citizenship Behavior: Its Nature and Antecedents," *Journal of Applied Psychology*, 68, pp. 653–663, 1983; and L. Van Dyne, J. W. Graham, and R. M. Dienesch, "Organizational Citizenship Behavior: Construct Redefinition, Measurement, and Validation," *Academy of Management Journal*, 37, pp. 765–802, 1994.

- Do we see a wide or narrow range in our scoring?
- What does this range suggest about our organization (or unit, if relevant)?
- In examining the individual behaviors, which ones have received a high rating? Which ones a low rating?
- What is the significance of any agreement on the high-rated items?
- What is the significance of any agreement on the low-rated items?
- What is most surprising about these scores?
- Which of the lower-rated items would you like to see more of?
- Which of the higher-rated items would you insist be retained?
- How can this organization induce a greater commitment on those items that we deem to be most important?
- What actions, if any, should we take to try to upgrade our own and our colleagues' commitment to this organization?

Meaning Making

According to the traditional view of leadership, the leaders of the organization articulate a vision that gives a sense of purpose to the organization. But can a vision be heartily adopted if the employees serve only as recipients of the vision? What happens if people in the organization don't subscribe to the espoused message? Will they be committed to carrying out a vision about which they have little say or that may not incorporate their local concerns?

There is an alternative to top-down vision creation. An organization's vision can preferably arise out of the group as it accomplishes its work. The position leader doesn't walk away to create the vision; the vision is often already present. It just needs articulation in the form of *meaning making*.

Within an organization, a meaning maker is someone who gives expression to what members of the group or organization are endeavoring to accomplish in their work together. He or she articulates a collective sense of what the group stands for. Meaning making can come from anyone in the group, though usually the meaning is voiced by someone who listens well, is close to the rhythm of the team, and is expressive. Especially when the organization as a whole or in its divisions is covering contested terrain or just facing uncertainty, meaning making can become a critical function because it can produce a cohering sense of purpose from what otherwise may appear foreign, vague, or even chaotic.

....

ACTIVITY 4.6

Meaning-Making Skills

The meaning maker can deploy a variety of techniques to articulate the organization's meaning, whether by portraying an image, by using humor, or by looking for patterns in a situation.

What makes the emergence of a meaning maker a leaderful occurrence is its egalitarian nature; anyone can become the meaning maker. The organization is not dependent on any one person to mobilize others to respond to a state of uncertainty or opportunity. Everyone can participate in the meaning-making process. However, certain individuals are more likely to emerge as meaning makers because they possess or develop explicit meaning-making skills.

STEP 1: Assemble a group of about eight learners who are interested in developing their meaning-making skills. The group could be an existing team or an ad hoc group. Ask them initially to think of a situation either in this team or unit or as part of another group when there was uncertainty or lack of agreement and the members were unclear on what was to be done.

STEP 2: Ask everyone to share his or her situation.

STEP 3: Pick one individual's situation as the case study for this activity.

STEP 4: Except for the individual whose situation has been chosen—call him or her the "principal"—group members should divide up the seven skills below, each taking one, and then spend ten minutes alone thinking about how he or she would apply the skill to the situation at hand. In your role as OD consultant, you may wish to make yourself available on an individual basis to explain the respective skill.

1. Looking for patterns in the situation
2. Personalizing the situation
3. Identifying what is missing or what isn't happening
4. Turning the problem upside down so that all the familiar parts look strange

5. Characterizing what the person is saying as an image or metaphor
6. Using humor to describe the situation
7. Synthesizing the facts

STEP 5: Begin a dialogue about the chosen situation, but except for the principal, each member represents the chosen skill. As the convener, make sure that each skill has been represented some three times before ending the dialogue.

STEP 6: Finish by debriefing the dialogue, considering the following questions:

1. For the principal, did this dialogue bring any coherence to a situation that was unclear or uncertain?
   a. What about the dialogue may have led to this result?
   b. Did any member's contribution(s) make a particularly significant impact?
2. For the other members, let them reveal the skill that they were attempting to emulate (you could also have the group try to guess initially).
   a. How did you experience this role?
   b. Was the skill natural or unnatural to you as a discussant?
3. If you haven't already, as the OD consultant, reveal the significance of the exercise as a way to gain some insight into the meaning-making function. Then, ask the group and the principal if greater meaning was brought to the situation at hand.
   a. What makes for a good meaning maker?
   b. How would you now evaluate the role of the meaning maker within the organization or within a group?
   c. What do you think gets in the way of one's organization or unit achieving greater meaning together?
   d. How can this organization increase its meaning making?

Worker Participation

There have long been movements in the domain of organizational democracy to instigate practices that involve workers more, both in workplace processes and outcomes. They come under various labels, such as worker participation, employee involvement, industrial democracy, or quality of work life (QWL). They vary in their expressions, from suggestions schemes, team briefings, and quality circles to work councils. They are related to leaderful practice when their designs suggest true participation through the inherent values of human dignity and autonomy. When these schemes are designed only to improve organizational performance, their application can become compromised and may be thought to be no more than tools by managers to induce greater work from their workers. Minimally, these practices should provide mutual gains to all parties.

....

ACTIVITY 4.7

Assessment of Worker Participation

In this activity, a list of possible features of worker participation will be displayed. In an OD capacity, you should first determine who might constitute a key team of decision makers or stakeholders, within the organization or organizational unit, who are interested in examining the issue of worker participation or employee involvement. This same team would be interested in effecting changes in policy and operations on the basis of this activity. In other words, those assembled would understand that this activity could serve as a gateway to a higher level of leaderful practices within the organization.

STEP 1: Once the team has been assembled, administer the survey instrument (displayed in Figure 4.4) either before holding a meeting to discuss the results or at the time of the meeting. In either instance, learners should receive some basic instruction on the nature of the worker participation movement and understand the logic behind the items listed in the survey.

STEP 2: Assemble the team after members have completed their survey. You can begin by saying that there is no correct score, except that higher scores are likely to be more predictive of leaderful practices. Total additive scores between 70 and 100 are worthy of note and are viewed favorably. After sharing total scores, the key part of this step is to view individual item scores. Members of the team make note of any items that received scores of 1 or 2 as well as those receiving scores of 5. If the team members are willing, have a full discussion of these item outliers, including these questions:

- Are the members agreeing on particular items at both extremes?
- How can they account for differences in their perceptions?

FIGURE **4.4**

A Survey Assessing Features of Worker Participation*

Instructions: Review each item and provide a rating, using the scale below, of the extent to which you believe this feature now characterizes the conditions of the workers in your organization (or organizational unit if that is your team's focus).

	5	4	3	2	1
	To a great extent	To a moderate extent	To a slight extent	Rarely	Not at all
1.	*Decision making*: Involvement in decision making			5 4 3 2 1	
2.	*Respect*: Treatment as a human being, with respect and dignity			5 4 3 2 1	
3.	*Learning and development*: Opportunity to pursue training			5 4 3 2 1	
4.	*Profit sharing*: Sharing in economic benefits			5 4 3 2 1	
5.	*Access*: Access to important information affecting their job and organization			5 4 3 2 1	
6.	*Pace*: Self-determination of the speed at which they work			5 4 3 2 1	
7.	*Security*: Sense of both physical and economic security			5 4 3 2 1	
8.	*Social relations*: Freedom to determine their own set of work relationships			5 4 3 2 1	
9.	*Equal opportunity*: Opportunity to advance and participate regardless of background			5 4 3 2 1	
10.	*Work space*: Adequate work space to do the job			5 4 3 2 1	
11.	*Autonomy*: Sense of being able to set their own work agenda			5 4 3 2 1	
12.	*Career aspirations*: Achievement of career goals beyond the job			5 4 3 2 1	
13.	*Trust*: Feeling that management will keep its promises			5 4 3 2 1	
14.	*Open door*: Opportunity to inform management about problems			5 4 3 2 1	
15.	*Work-family balance*: Understanding by management that workers have to meet their family obligations			5 4 3 2 1	

(Continued on next page)

FIGURE **4.4** *(Continued)*

16.	*Advancement*: Promotion based on ability, performance, and experience	5 4 3 2 1
17.	*Working hours*: Ability to set their own working time, including breaks, overtime, and time off	5 4 3 2 1
18.	*Stress*: Absence of undue work demands or pressure	5 4 3 2 1
19.	*Confidence in management*: Sense that management is aware of and concerned about their needs and interests	5 4 3 2 1
20.	*Work group*: Feeling that one's work group provides mutual support and encouragement	5 4 3 2 1
21.	*Supervisors*: Working relationships with supervisors reflect fairness, mutual respect and honesty	5 4 3 2 1
22.	*Power distance*: Gap in power between managers and workers is narrow	5 4 3 2 1
23.	*Work quality*: Work deemed interesting and enjoyable	5 4 3 2 1

* Adapted from scales in the domains of quality of work life (QWL), employee involvement (EI), and total quality management (TQM), such as from: E. Miller, "Measuring the Quality of Work Life in General Motors: Interview with Howard C. Carlson," *Personnel*, 55, pp. 24–25, 1978; and B. F. Daily and J. W. Bishop, "TQM Workforce Factors and Employee Involvement: The Pivotal Role of Teamwork," *Journal of Management Issues*, 15, pp. 393–412, 2003.

- What do the low-rated items say about the organization (or unit)?
- What do the high-rated items suggest?
- Are there any surprises in these ratings?
- Can the group agree on the items most in need of development, and those most in need of retention?

STEP 3: Continue the dialogue by focusing on what would need to be changed in the organization to improve some of the low-rated items. Discuss whether there is readiness to change. Would workers and managers both be receptive to a change? Finish by talking through any specific steps that members of the team can make to begin planning and implementing any changes suggested by this activity.

....

CASE STUDY

Cultural Change at Scientific Research Administration

LEONARD GLICK

Background

A leading research organization launched several reengineering projects aimed at significantly reducing its administrative costs. This case deals with the project that focused on the repair and maintenance of its approximately sixty buildings. In doing so, we combined sociotechnical system (high-performance work system) and reengineering methodologies. The key goal was to streamline the work processes and implement management practices that would foster the commitment of the workforce through collaborative practices. Said another way, the goal was to create an organization that encouraged leaderful behavior.

We formed a cross-functional, cross-hierarchical organizational design team consisting of front-line (unionized) trades workers (plumbers, electricians, and so on), supervisors, managers, and customers. This design team met three days a week for several weeks. They followed a comprehensive process in which they investigated, analyzed, and discussed the various components and outcomes of the current organization, such as the work flow, organizational structure, and reward system. One fundamental assumption was that the new organization be designed as a system with interdependent components that should "fit" together. The team's role was to question everything and propose a "reengineered organization" that would lead to lower costs and higher quality.

As a consultant to the team, I had many roles. One was as expert on the design process overall and on the content of its components. Another was as a facilitator who encouraged the members to challenge the existing system and each other. The design team was officially led by a team "captain," but the climate was very democratic. Front-line workers challenged their managers and supervisors and vice versa. Anyone could—and did—propose ideas.

The Culture

Through its data gathering, analyses, and deliberations, the design team surfaced several problems. For example, much time and money was spent on waiting, non-value-added administrative work, handoffs and approvals, and ineffectual coordination. Among the outcomes were high costs, slow response, and dissatisfied customers. Solving these problems would require major changes in the entire system; for example, its structure, jobs, work flow, and culture.

In light of these problems, the design team proposed some features for a redesign. They included:

- A more decentralized organization
- Empowered teams, composed of many trades, responsible for the maintenance of "their" buildings
- More flexible job descriptions
- Greatly reduced handoffs, paperwork, and supervisor approvals
- More transparency about costs and performance
- Direct communication between the workers and the customers

The remainder of this case describes the process used to analyze the existing culture and to design and implement a new culture based on the redesign.

The Process for Cultural Assessment and Cultural Redesign

Describe the Current Culture (Enacted Values)

We invited about twenty additional members of the organization and five to ten customers to participate. After explaining that the goal was to describe the current culture—that is, the enacted values—we formed small groups and asked them to discuss questions like:

- What do people get rewarded for?
- What do people get in trouble for?
- How would you describe the typical repair or maintenance worker?
- How would you describe the current repair process?
- If a Martian observed your organization, what would he or she notice?
- Think of a few incidents or stories that you think illustrate the "essence" of this organization.
- Describe the experience of being a customer, worker, or manager.

Groups then shared their answers as other groups confirmed, disagreed, or elaborated. There were some points on which there was consensus. We captured these, attempting to pinpoint the underlying belief or value. There were some areas for which there was less agreement, and these required more debate. The total process took an afternoon. Here are some of the clear enacted values that emerged:

- Work is done as individuals.
- Someone else tells you what to do.
- External controls are needed.
- No one owns the problem.
- We react to the customer.
- Costs are someone else's problem.

Assess the Current Culture

In a separate meeting, the design team assessed the current culture—particularly in relation to the key principles, goals, and direction of the partially completed redesign. The questions discussed included:

- How well do the current enacted values fit with our redesign?
- Do these enacted values help or hinder achieving the organization's goals?

Because it was obvious that the current enacted values clashed with the redesign and would hinder results, the key question became:

- What enacted values would be needed to support the design components and enable achievement of the business goals?

Specify the Desired Culture

The design team debated the question: What values would support the redesign; that is, what culture did they need? Considering their redesign principles and choices concerning work, rewards, technology, development, and the organizational results they wanted, they espoused a new set of values, including:

- Teams outperform individuals.
- Decisions should be made at the lowest competent level.
- Employees can be trusted.
- Teams should "own" the solution.
- Problems should be anticipated.
- Everyone should work to reduce costs.

Note that these values are fully consistent with leaderful behavior in that they empower the workforce and form teams that are responsible for self-management, problem solving, and high-quality work.

Table 4.1 presents the contrast in the two sets of values.

TABLE **4.1**

Differences Between the Enacted and Espoused Values

Current Enacted Values	Future Espoused Values
Work is done as individuals	Teams outperform individuals
Someone else tells you what to do	Decisions should be made at the lowest competent level
External controls are needed	Employees can be trusted
No one owns the problem	Teams should "own" the solution
We react to the customer	Problems should be anticipated
Costs are someone else's problem	Everyone should work to reduce costs

Identify Ways to Enact the Espoused Values

In light of the sharp contrast, the team discussed how to transform the culture—to move *from* the existing enacted values *to* the espoused desired values. It would require both employees and managers learning new skills, changes in organizational practices and design, ongoing feedback, and physical changes, among others. Several ideas had already been discussed by the design team. Here are some examples of what was implemented:

- Structure the organization into cross-functional (trades) teams, responsible for a group of buildings and their occupants.
- Rotate "leadership" of the teams.
- Post the values (make them visible) and encourage people to raise the question, "How well are we enacting them—both good and counter examples?"
- Change the role of "traditional supervisor" to "team coach."
- Provide a clinic for new coaches in which they discuss real issues and situations and how to deal with them in ways consistent with the values.
- Begin the day with a team meeting to decide priorities and assignments and report on work done as needed.
- Provide more information, including costs, to all team members.
- Track and discuss quality and costs regularly.
- Develop the practice of looking around and asking customers about likely future needs when making a repair.

- Eliminate punching in.
- Provide training for employees and supervisors.

Even with all of these initiatives and more, the results were mixed. Some teams made substantial progress in enacting the values, and others were less successful. There were several explanations for the mixed results. First were the skills and style of the coach—specifically the ability to "let go" and encourage leaderful behavior. Second, some trades workers were more or less accepting of the notion of working with others. Third, union contracts prevented some organizational changes (job descriptions, pay systems) that would have supported the redesign. Fourth, some physical arrangements, such as team space, were more conducive to the redesign. Fifth, some managers were less supportive of the management philosophy (values) embedded in the redesign. Sixth, a significant subset of the larger organization, Scientific Research Administration, was either indifferent or opposed to this approach. Seventh, organizational and cultural changes of this magnitude require constant vigilance and renewal. Indifferent management, budget constraints, and new priorities can impede and reverse progress.

Chapter Five

Network-Level Change

L IFE IN ORGANIZATIONS HAS BECOME MORE COMPLEX because bound-aries have become more permeable. In order to accomplish our work within a knowledge economy, we need to rely on a range of stakeholders, many of whom operate outside the organization's borders. Indeed, life in the twenty-first century is becoming increasingly networked whereby we may begin to think of ourselves as parties to webs of partnerships. Social networks, in turn, are typically characterized by collaborative practices in which the parties learn to share resources in ways that are mutual to the participating entities.

There are always cases in which one of the institutional members of the network mobilizes the participation of others, but most social networks are self-organizing, resulting in members participating to further their self- and collective interests. We have given the name "weavers" to designate those individuals who play a critical role not only to organize networks but to sustain them once formed. Network weavers work with others to mobilize and to document exchanges within the network. Using tools such as social network analysis (SNA), weavers can point out where there are gaps in knowledge resources, where bottlenecks may be occurring within communication patterns, where access to new resources may be necessary, where special expertise may be required, or where clusters of connections may be formed from which the network can learn.

The process of change at the network level is dynamic and not as con-trollable as was the conventional bureaucracy. Sharing among network members is often emergent rather than planned. Variety and adaptability take the place of efficiency to allow for continuous change. What holds the network together is social capital based as much on trust as on rules and regulations. From trust evolves a sense of shared meaning making, which is what mobilizes the creation of new knowledge.

The prior levels of change discussed in this fieldbook instigate the necessary competencies for networks to flourish. At the individual level, learners become more reflective and more aware of their cultural assumptions; at the interpersonal level, they dedicate themselves to inquire more with others; at the team level, they become more committed to supporting teammates while performing the work of the team; and at the organizational level, they begin to identify systemic patterns and advocate for change. When successful, members of the network exhibit what we might call "network citizenship behavior," or special efforts made on behalf of their network over and above routine network services.

The seven activities in this chapter are designed to help prospective and current network weavers develop their skills to form and nourish social networks in ways that produce the necessary collaborative behavior that can sustain the network over time.

The first activity, **Stakeholder Dialogue**, provides a means for learners to develop a stakeholder list and subsequently to organize it by impact. Then, learners are invited to practice the necessary dialogic skills to engage their stakeholders in productive discourse.

The second activity, **Critical Moments Reflection**, introduces the "Critical Moments" strategy to help network participants verbally and graphically represent some of the key moments or changes that have helped define the community and use the data to uncover some of the cultural assumptions that may need deeper exploration.

The third activity, **Network Citizenship Behavior Questionnaire**, introduces the concept of network citizenship behavior as actions taken by network participants over and above normal operating behavior and assesses its magnitude within the network.

The fourth activity, **Questions for Network Weaver Role Development**, features a self-assessment in the form of twenty questions to assist current or prospective network weavers scrutinize some of the critical strategies and proclivities that make for effective performance.

The fifth activity, **The Ten Lessons for Managing Networks**, considers the role of the network manager and prescribes a set of ten lessons to serve as the basis for dialogue with stakeholders to access information, exchange resources, and solve problems occurring at the boundaries of one's own organization.

The sixth activity, **The Four Dimensions of Quality in Network Relationships**, outlines four specific steps to building quality relationships in social networks and then suggests and solicits some interventions that can be made to enhance the value of network engagements.

The seventh activity, **The Seven Core Principles for Effective Public Engagement**, presents a set of principles for evaluating the democratic quality of network decision making. The principles are followed by a set of practices that network members are asked to both do *less* of and *more* of in order to bolster network public engagement.

Stakeholder Relations

Stakeholders are people or institutions in your prospective network who are affected by or can affect the course of any project or set of projects in which you are involved. In Activity 5.1, called "Stakeholder Dialogue," learners first identify who their key stakeholders are, assess their interests, and begin to formulate a strategy for engagement. After completing the analysis, learners can develop a strategy to draw out the interests of their potential stakeholders, identify relations between them, spot conflicts of interest, and assess the best way to involve them. Then, they engage selected stakeholders using some of the best tools at our disposal to produce useful dialogue.

....

ACTIVITY 5.1

Stakeholder Dialogue

This activity could be initiated as an individual reflective exercise, but in due course learners should work on it with colleagues who also participate in the network in question. The first steps help organize a new network or analyze an emerging or existing network. The approach taken is merely a formal method to capture the positioning of one's stakeholders at a given point in time, acknowledging that networks are fluid structures.

STEP 1: Identify the learner's stakeholders by drawing up a list. Organize the list by using whatever categories might be most helpful. Here are some examples of useful categories:

- Formal position, such as title
- Demographics, such as gender or age or seniority
- Primary versus secondary, based on the degree of direct involvement
- Internal versus external, based on whether or not they are in the same organization, and if so, whether they are above, below, or at your same level
- Function, on the basis of their potential role in your project, such as advocate, knowledge resource, project implementer, or evaluator

STEP 2: Next, learners develop a stakeholder strategy matrix, a prototype of which is displayed in Table 5.1. The strategy matrix guides learners involved in a prospective engagement with selected stakeholders. Stakeholders can have an impact on a project because of their influence—the power they may have to control or facilitate key decisions—and/or because of their importance—their ability to bring to bear critical resources or energy to make things happen. In

TABLE **5.1**

Stakeholder Strategy Matrix

Stakeholder	Proposed Impact	What You Need from Them	What They Need from You	How You Plan to Meet Your Mutual Needs

turn, stakeholders with high impact may not immediately choose to participate in a project, may have a conflict with the learner or with another key stakeholder, or may even negatively affect the project unless they see the learner's interests as mutual with their own.

STEP 3: Now learners should be prepared to engage in a stakeholder dialogue. Learners get into trios, working with two other close colleagues who may or may not be part of the learner's network. This step is designed to help a learner (whom we'll call the principal) prepare for a dialogue with one of his or her key stakeholders who previously was identified as having an impact on the learner's projects. The second colleague in the trio takes on the role of the stakeholder whom the learner would like to involve productively in the project. Thus, the weaver managing the activity should give the learner sufficient time to brief the colleague in the stakeholder role about his or her position, needs, function, and impact. The third colleague performs the observer role, using the observer sheet included as Figure 5.1. The points to be observed represent some of the canons of productive dialogue, many of which were introduced in prior chapters

FIGURE **5.1**

Observer Sheet for Stakeholder Dialogue

Instructions: During the dialogue, did the principal display the following dialogic skills? (Please take notes and be prepared to provide feedback at the end of the activity.)

Actively listen? Paid attention to what the other person said and to the underlying emotional and thematic subtexts of what was said. Did he or she allow for pauses and let the person fully speak?

Invite inquiry? Gently asked rather than required answers.

Give sensitive feedback? Asked permission before giving feedback.

(Continued on next page)

FIGURE **5.1** *(Continued)*

Develop trust? Provided a sense of psychological safety.
Display compassion? Showed empathy rather than neutrality.
Clarify assumptions? Revealed assumptions for the stakeholder to see.
Demonstrate provisionality? Considered points of view to be hypotheses to be examined.
Go "meta"? Noticed when there was something important happening in the dynamics in the moment.
Reveal intentions? Was clear in what he or she needed and held no hidden intents.
Follow the energy? Tuned in to what was alive for the other.

of this fieldbook. They should be explained to the learner and will be brought out during the feedback debriefing to be held after the role play. During the feedback session, have both observer and colleague in role participate actively in the debriefing with the learner.

··

Network Stories

Although the tools of social network analysis have become very sophisticated in pointing out the structure of a network, we are more concerned in this fieldbook with personal and collective agency—what did people do that made a difference. One way to probe into the underlying dynamics of the emerging relationships within social networks is to find out about the stories that personify the formal and informal exchanges or relationships between people. The stories, often enhanced through visual imagery, carry the local knowledge that mobilizes the reason for collaborating. Further, stories enable practitioners to question the assumptions and even biases about other network members that, in turn, may influence outcomes for the community. Equipped with this deeper information, practitioners strengthen their capacity to improvise and innovate, to respond to complex interrelationships more effectively, and to incorporate personal knowledge during the process of network development.

··

ACTIVITY 5.2

Critical Moments Reflection

The Critical Moments strategy was invented at MIT's Center for Reflective Community Practice (now called the Community Innovators Lab) as a methodology to support practitioners in various community settings in uncovering, building, and valuing the knowledge they have gained from their practice.[18] It has since been applied in a number of diverse settings and can be particularly useful as an activity to clarify roles, facilitate collaboration, and surface some of the underlying assumptions within a social network.

---

[18] See C. L. McDowell, A. Nagel, S. M. Williams, and C. Canepa, "Building Knowledge from the Practice of Local Communities," *Knowledge Management for Development Journal*, 1, pp. 30–40, 2005; and J. Amulya, "Summary of Critical Moments Reflection," Center for Reflective Community Practice Working Paper 2004–06 (Cambridge, MA: MIT, 2004).

STEP 1: Assemble a team of participants from an existing social network, but try not to exceed fifteen people. If the network is larger, divide up the group, or though not ideal, allow each of the participating institutions to nominate representatives to participate. Prior to the meeting, agree on the frame or inquiry question that the team will work on. Consider an open question that upon resolution would advance the participants' sense of efficacy over their work.

STEP 2: With everyone present, confirm the question and also a time frame over which the question has prevailed (especially if the network has gone through multiple cycles of experience). Ask each member present to privately think about a "critical moment," positive or negative, that addresses the question and that was important in advancing or setting back the work of the network. The critical moment classification could be broadened to characterize the moment "that defined the community" during the given time period. Another variant is to propose the so-called Most Significant Change (MSC) approach used by Rick Davies and Jess Dart.[19] The question in this instance would be, "What do you consider to be 'the most significant change that took place' in the network over a specific time period?"

STEP 3: Each member shares his or her critical moment verbally and, if desired, graphically, perhaps even including a timeline. After everyone has finished, note collectively whether the selected moments are similar or different and allow some time for a discussion of what the selections say about the community. Why, if this were the case, did the critical moments end up so disperse? What surprised members about their selection?

STEP 4: The team selects the one (or more, if time) critical moment that it believes offers the most insight into the inquiry question. As the weaver, engage the team in a full dialogue about the critical moment and its significance to the community in shaping the inquiry question. Network members use this time to pose a number of questions that may surface some of the underlying issues; such as:

- How does this story symbolically depict our community?
- What assumptions, contradictions, or paradoxes does it bring up?
- What are the questions that it raises that need to be addressed?
- What does it say about how the issue of authority or leadership is being handled?

---

[19] R. Davies and J. Dart, *The "Most Significant Change" (MSC) Technique: A Guide to Its Use*, *www.mande.co.uk/docs/MSCGuide.htm*, 2005. Retrieved December 21, 2009.

- How is the vital issue of trust being viewed?
- Are there cultural issues that need to be addressed?

STEP 5: If more than one reflection team has been assembled, bring the teams together and share stories. If the teams have worked on the same question, what insights might be drawn from the ways they have handled the question? If they worked on a different question, what new knowledge should be shared with the full community to advance its agenda?

STEP 6: Debrief the activity by together identifying any lessons learned and the implications for addressing the inquiry question and moving the work of the network forward.

....

Network Citizenship Behavior

The concept of network citizenship behavior (NCB) is derived from the more familiar term, organizational citizenship behavior (OCB), referred to in chapter 1, signifying actions taken by employees that, though not recognized by the formal reward system, are performed anyway to help an individual, group, or organization. The literature on OCB has differentiated the object of the citizenship behavior as other individuals (for example, willingly giving time to help others who have work-related problems) or the group or organization as a whole (for example, attending to functions that are not required but that help the organization's image). There has also been recent work suggesting that citizenship behavior can occur as a group-level phenomenon (for example, the people in my work group are willing to put in extra time on the job). In this activity, we introduce the concept of network citizenship behavior as activities on the part of members of a social network to contribute to the viability and success of the network over and above their involvement in regular network services. Members and organizations are typically involved in more than one network, so sustaining commitment is a critical function that can be shaped by the network weaver.

. . . .

ACTIVITY 5.3

Network Citizenship Behavior Questionnaire

The questionnaire in Figure 5.2 was developed by the author based on items used in OCB surveys,[20] but it is directed toward explicit *network* behaviors. Used here predominantly as a survey feedback mechanism, it can also be used for research purposes—for example, as a pre-post survey following any intervention to improve network functioning.

STEP 1: Distribute the questionnaire to all identified nodes (involved members or organizations) in the network and ask them to fill it out either in person or online, and return it to a central processor. Summarize the statistical information, using frequency charts and content analysis, and prepare a report based on the findings.

STEP 2: Assemble the network, asking for as full attendance as possible. Present the summary findings and report and point out any findings of interest (positive, negative, or neutral). The community should make a decision whether or not to reveal the names of those having taken the survey. In either the anonymous or disclosed condition, discuss the findings as a group. What is the overall level of NCB in this community? Consider each item individually and, again referring to the findings, discuss together whether more or less could or should be done to advance the goals and operation of the community. In addition, consider:

- What could be done individually to improve the community's NCB?
- What could be done collectively to improve it?
- What activities are being undertaken now that should be encouraged or discouraged?
- Is the network having a sufficient effect at the policy level?
- What changes should be made to improve the community's overall functioning?

STEP 3: As the network weaver, you may wish initially to reflect privately on the survey feedback meeting to determine whether there are additional steps to be made to improve the citizenship behavior of network participants. Invite your close colleagues to serve as sounding boards and to augment the

---

[20] See, for example, K. Lee and N. J. Allen, "Organizational Citizenship Behavior and Workplace Deviance: The Role of Affect and Cognitions," *Journal of Applied Psychology*, 87, pp. 131–42, 2002.

FIGURE **5.2**

Network Citizenship Behavior Questionnaire

Name of Network: _____

A. Answer each question thinking about your membership in this network (using the scale below):

Not at All	A Little	A Moderate Amount	A Lot	All the Time
1	2	3	4	5

Relative to this network, to what extent do you:

1.	Attend to functions that are not required but that help the network's mission	1 2 3 4 5
2.	Keep up with activities in the network	1 2 3 4 5
3.	Keep abreast of policy developments that concern the network	1 2 3 4 5
4.	Willingly represent the network in public	1 2 3 4 5
5.	Offer ideas to improve the functioning of the network	1 2 3 4 5
6.	Seek to increase the reach of this network	1 2 3 4 5
7.	Take action to protect the network from potential problems	1 2 3 4 5
8.	Develop your own expertise in the network domain	1 2 3 4 5
9.	Seek a leadership role within the network	1 2 3 4 5

B. Some of the explicit network activities in which you have engaged are:

a. At the policy level:

b. At the operating level:

reflective process. Following are some considerations that might be brought into this concluding dialogue and potentially into subsequent network exchanges:

- Do the network nodes have sufficient citizenship toward this network, and if not, what are some of the barriers?
- Do they have sufficient resources both from their own organization as well as from the network to participate actively?
- Are they sufficiently informed about the goals and operation of this network?
- Is the purpose of the network kept alive and reviewed to be sure it is still meeting the pressing needs of its membership?
- Is there a means for any disagreements or conflicts to be surfaced and effectively resolved?
- Is the network as a whole being effectively managed? If not, should there be a consideration of alternative network management structures?

The Network Weaver Role

Although social networks have been around for centuries, our formal attention to them has been recent and thus we tend to know less about the weaver role than about the other agency roles. Perhaps the key to the weaver role derives from its meaning as establishing connections among people, helping them to build strong trusting relationships. The role of the weaver differs depending upon whether the social network is loosely organized as a means to provide information to its membership or tightly coupled as a means to accomplish mutual work—or someplace in between. In either case, the weaver needs to have the capacity to bring people together so that they find value in contributing their time and resources to the network.

Weavers may occupy formal roles within the network or may emerge informally or as needed to strengthen network ties. In either case, there are questions that they can ask themselves to help assess how to best support the networks to which they already belong or the ones that they want to help create.

....

ACTIVITY 5.4

Questions for Network Weaver Role Development

The weaver role, like the prior change agent roles, relies on agency, meaning that its occupants facilitate change but are not responsible for doing all the change on their own. They highlight the mission, or what may be called the "collective value proposition," of the network and carry out a number of functions to ensure that the network continues to serve the greater good of the participating members.

This activity offers a series of questions to consider when thinking about how to carry out a network weaver role. The questions are informed by a number of resources, including *Net Gains: A Handbook of Network Builders* by Peter Plastrik and Madeleine Taylor,[21] the community weaving work of Cheryl Honey,[22] and practitioner accounts from Rosa Zubizarreta,[23] Steve Waddell,[24] June Holley,[25] and others.

STEP 1: Choose a specific network to keep in mind as you explore each of the questions to follow. Try to focus on a network of which you are currently a member, whether it is a formal network or a more informal one. If you are not able to think of a current network, you might choose one to which you belonged in the past or one that you would like to help create in the future.

In any case, you will receive more value from this activity by working through the ensuing questions with a specific network in mind. Once you have chosen a network to work with, you will find that some of these questions are more relevant or more challenging than others. That is to be expected, since each network has its own history and purpose in addition to its own areas of strength and areas of need.

STEP 2: The following series of questions—organized by some key network functions—are designed to help you think through the network weaver role more carefully. As you consider each question, you may want to use a journal to elaborate on some of your responses. If there are questions you are not able to answer at this point, they might serve as jumping-off points for further learning.

---

[21] P. Plastrik and M. Taylor, *Net Gains: A Handbook of Network Builders*, *www.barrfoundation.org/resources/resources_show.htm?doc_id=436179*. Retrieved December 21, 2009.

[22] See *www.familynetwork.org/*. Retrieved December 21, 2009.

[23] See *www.diapraxis.com/index.html*. Retrieved December 21, 2009.

[24] See *www.networkingaction.net/*. Retrieved December 21, 2009.

[25] See *http://networkweaver.blogspot.com/*. Retrieved December 21, 2009.

That learning may involve general theory and accounts about networks, local knowledge or "insider expertise" from informants within your network, or some combination of both. In addition, if there are roles or functions that you see need filling but are outside of your current capabilities, consider whether others in the network may be able to help.

Membership and Purpose

1. Who is this network meant to serve? Identify both existing and potential members of the network. What do they need *from* the network and what may they provide *for* the network? What different *kinds* of stakeholders are there, either actually or potentially? How might their needs and gifts differ?

2. You may discover some "co-weavers" who are interested in starting a new network or in strengthening an existing one. What are their views about how they would like the network to better serve its members?

3. What current visions do the members of this network have about how the network might best serve them? (Both this question and some of the others are worth revisiting from time to time, as the network grows and develops.)

4. What are the strategies and functions that will help the network accomplish its purpose? How are these functions performed, and by whom?

Structure, Communication, and Relationships

5. What structures need to be in place to support communication and relationships between members? In what ways are these structures working well? In what ways might they be improved?

6. How can you provide new or existing network members with information regarding the purpose, strategies, functions, and structure of the network? How might they offer input with regard to changing strategies, new functions, or alternative structures that might be desirable?

7. How can you ensure that network members have all of the information they need to participate effectively in the network? How might network members easily access information about one another's relevant needs and interests so that they can collaborate more effectively?

Supporting Leadership and Inclusivity

8. How might you support the "hubs" in the network, namely, those members who are well connected to others?

9. How might you encourage the emergence of other critical roles, such as experts, mentors, and innovators?

10. How might you support potential connections that are currently being overlooked or underutilized?

11. How might you help members connect to new ideas and resources at different levels: within their smaller clusters, across clusters, within the whole network, and outside of the network within the larger community?

Trouble Shooting

12. How can you tell if a network bottleneck is forming? What might be causing it? What might help resolve it?

13. How might you create and use network maps and other tools to visually show the ties in the network, to help develop strategies for improving or creating connections, and enhance the development and dissemination of new knowledge?

14. How might you update and redesign the information management systems and structures in the network to keep up with the network's ongoing growth and development?

Development and Sustainability

15. How might you expand the network through the use of more complex network structures (such as multi-hub) and leadership?

16. How might you monitor the network's financial health and support fundraising efforts as necessary? Is the lack of financing holding back a critical goal?

Evaluation and Course Correction

17. How will you measure the effectiveness of the network's short- and long-term growth and vitality? Consider assessing such attributes as the *resilience* of the network (whether it is dependent on a small or large number of individuals) and its *diversity* (whether individuals are interacting with those like or different from them) and seek to adjust these as necessary.

18. How might you determine whether the network is starting to veer away from its original or developing mission? What indicators might be useful to look for?

19. If the network is indeed veering away from the original mission, what factors might encourage you and others to attempt to adapt the original mission? What factors might encourage you and others to attempt to return to the original mission?

STEP 3: The final question is multipronged because it refers to the personal and professional elements that current research suggests contribute to effectiveness in the weaver role. Continuing to work with your colleagues and mentors, you may wish to journal about the attributes listed below to assess and develop your weaver capabilities.

20. As a network weaver, to what degree do you possess some or all of the following:

- Passion for the process of helping people connect and interact
- Interest in knowing and introducing people with varying perspectives and backgrounds
- Talent in helping others develop trust through productive collaboration
- Commitment in helping people work through differences and conflicts
- Capacity to facilitate or to enable others to do the work
- Willingness to get one's hands wet when needed—to be a "doer"
- Proclivity to multi-task or keep multiple balls in the air at once
- Ability to implement and follow through
- System-level thinking—can see the big picture and detect patterns
- Abstract thinking—can work with knowledge as a resource
- Good time management skills
- Self-motivation and self-starting ability
- Comfort with ambiguity

Network Management

As suggested at the outset of this chapter, managing networks is different from standard administrative management within traditional hierarchical organizations. In particular, in social networks, trust, knowledge, and consensus replace hierarchical authority, decisions are as much brokered as made and passed down a chain of command, network structures are likely to be self-organizing, and connections are as likely to be made through information technology as through face-to-face meetings. In addition, we know that the search for knowledge-based solutions in most organizations is likely to take place as much outside as inside the current organizational apparatus. Learning how to take advantage of knowledge opportunities out-side one's familiar boundaries has become a source not only of competitive advantage, but in some cases of survival itself. Thus, managing networks will become an increasingly important competency for professional staffs in organizations across all sectors—private, public, and not-for-profit.

....

ACTIVITY 5.5

The Ten Lessons for Managing Networks

This activity is derived from a set of lessons produced in a study called *Leveraging Networks* under the direction of Robert Agranoff[26] in which public managers reported how their work required contact with other agencies to access infor-mation, exchange resources, and solve problems occurring at the boundaries of their own agencies. These lessons, reproduced in Table 5.2, can be used by network weavers across a range of social networks to monitor their own or oth-ers' management of current network communities.

STEP 1: Initially review Table 5.2 by yourself and become familiar with the ten lessons. Then, determine whether these lessons of network management apply primarily to you as the network weaver or to one of your clients who indeed may be serving as the network manager (though perhaps under a different alias) for the community in question. If you are the network weaver and concurrently also the network manager, you might wish to invite some colleagues who are members of the community in question to join you for a wide-open dialogue about your performance of these ten critical points. If you are advising a network manager, plan a coaching session with him or her to share and review each one of these lessons to determine whether they are important to the network, and if so, whether they are being fulfilled either by the manager or by someone else serving in a hub or managerial capacity.

STEP 2: If you are working with a network manager, after reviewing these lessons with him or her, invite the manager to assemble some of the key participants in the network for a reflective session on the process of network management. If the manager decides to use the "Ten Lessons" as a basis for the dialogue, Table 5.2 could be shared with these participants in advance. Once assembled, the team should review each of the lessons and determine, if they are applicable,

---

[26] R. Agranoff, *Leveraging Networks* (Washington, DC: IBM Center for the Business of Governments, 2003).

TABLE **5.2**

The Ten Lessons for Managing Networks*

Number	Lesson	Significance
1.	Represent your agency as well as the network	Unless you are working as an external consultant, be sure that as a network manager you are representing your agency's interests while also contributing to the vitality of the network as a whole
2.	Step up to the administrative duties	It is far too easy to overlook some of the critical administrative burdens, such as arranging meetings—be they online or in person—keeping records of proceedings, bringing in outside experts, or managing the software requirements
3.	Focus the agenda	Since everyone is busy, members need reinforcement, such as by having a work plan with real issues on the agenda, that they are part of a serious collaborative body, and that their time is precious
4.	Recognize that your leadership is shared	The network manager can never have all the answers so must rely on the expertise of the full community and in some cases reach out beyond the current set of clusters
5.	Stay within the network's decision bounds	Unless the network is a "production" network that makes operating decisions for itself, don't trample on the authority of your members' institutions or you might compromise their standing
6.	Use collaborative decision making	No member, including the network manager, can force any issue so be prepared for a protracted dialogue on especially knotty issues
7.	Be creative	Since the whole is often bigger than the sum of the parts, participants must engage in joint learning and experimentation
8.	Have patience	With no ultimate authority residing in any one person but the need to solicit node involvement and agreement, you need to be patient and "wait for the teachable moment"
9.	Recruit continually	Do not cease to recruit new blood to the community, reaching out to stakeholders, and even to prospective opponents, beyond the network so as to be inclusive and to keep learning

(Continued on next page)

TABLE **5.2** *(Continued)*

Number	Lesson	Significance
10.	Use intrinsic incentives	Emphasize the intrinsic value from involvement, especially the chance to expand participants' knowledge base or to be part of something bigger than themselves

*Adapted from Robert Agranoff, *Leveraging Networks* (Washington: IBM Center for the Business of Governments, 2003).

whether they are being observed by the network manager, and if so, at what level of performance. Be sure to indicate that it is not always the manager's prerogative to fulfill each "lesson," in which case, the assembled team might decide whose role it may be and how it is to be accomplished. Be sure to engage the team in a further dialogue about any changes to be made within the network to improve its effectiveness along the lines of this activity.

The Quality of Knowledge Relationships

Social networks can become particularly valuable in helping people access knowledge that may not be otherwise available to them but that could be critical in helping them perform their work. In fact, many of us in the workplace are more inclined to turn to our friends and colleagues for answers than to other sources of information such as a database or file cabinet. Yet, some contacts seem to help us more than others, suggesting that it's not as much a question of how many people we know in our social networks as it is the quality of the relationships that we maintain.

As a weaver, you can help members of networks and communities improve their relationships by helping them gain access and build trust among their contacts.

··

ACTIVITY 5.6

The Four Dimensions of Quality in Network Relationships

Based on the research of Rob Cross, Andrew Parker, and Stephen Borgatti,[27] four dimensions were found to be critical in developing social networks that would furnish a high level of knowledge creation and application:

1. Knowing what others know
2. Gaining timely access
3. Establishing a productive engagement
4. Learning from a safe relationship

The steps in this activity explain these four dimensions and suggest coaching and facilitating strategies to augment their use.

STEP 1: Familiarize yourself with the four dimensions to building quality relationships in the social network(s) in which you may be serving in a weaver capacity.

1. *Knowing what others know.* Before pursuing a contact with others, it is important to have a sense of the relevance of their knowledge, skills, and abilities relative to the problem at hand. It is often surprising that at times we are unaware of the hidden expertise of even our close colleagues. In other instances, there may be people whom we don't know, or don't know well, who in the end possess the critical information that could advance our projects.

2. *Gaining timely access.* It's not enough just to identify those who can provide knowledge resources; it is just as essential to gain access to them in a timely manner. Impediments such as gaps in power and authority or physical and technical distance might affect the likelihood of being consulted.

3. *Establishing a productive engagement.* It's often not sufficient to merely exchange information with colleagues; it is just as important to engage with them to think through the problem at hand. The focal person in this instance may need someone who is willing to take the time to listen first

---

[27] R. Cross, A. Parker, and S. P. Borgatti, *A Bird's-Eye View: Using Social Network Analysis to Improve Knowledge Creation and Sharing* (Somers, NY: IBM Institute for Business Values, 2002).

and sincerely try to understand the issue and its full implications, including any connection between the person and the problem.

4. *Learning from a safe relationship.* Just requesting information, particularly when roles and authority come into play, can expose an individual's vulnerability. Thus, relationships should be initiated and fulfilled on the basis of trust. A sense of psychological safety in a relationship also provides room for enhanced creativity and learning.

STEP 2: Assemble members of the network, on both an individual and a team basis, and provide coaching along these four dimensions. You should feel free to raise such issues as:

- What is the quality of the relationships that you maintain in your community?
- Do you have timely access to people who can meet your knowledge needs?
- What gets in the way of successful contact?
- Are your interactions productive and are your contacts sensitive to your needs?
- What would make these interactions more effective?
- Would you say that your network relationships are characterized by psychological safety and trust?

STEP 3: Continuing to work with both individuals and with teams of key stakeholders or even with the current full community (if it isn't overly large), complete Table 5.3 together. In this table, the four dimensions of quality relationships are listed in the first column; the objectives of quality relationships in the second; and advisable interventions to improve the fulfillment of each dimension in the third column. Some prototypical interventions have been denoted, but you should fill in the third column with your own set of suggestions for improving the quality of the knowledge relationships in your community.

TABLE **5.3**

Improving the Quality of Relationships in the Network*

Dimension	Objectives	Needed Interventions
Knowledge	Increase awareness of key stakeholders' knowledge, skills, and abilities	• Nurture communities of practice • Create platforms for archiving codified knowledge • •
Access	Assess speed of access to key stakeholders and diagnose any blockages on the part of both inquirer and source	• Form and facilitate peer feedback sessions • Conduct surveys and/or social network analyses • •
Engagement	Improve the dynamics of network exchanges by promoting real engagement	• Sponsor communications workshops • Widely disseminate and teach the use of interactive tools, such as synchronous technologies or white boarding • •
Safety	Support the development of trust in network relationships	• Hold informal face-to-face sessions, such as "brown bag" lunches • Provide coaching to peers who wish to improve their professional relationships • •

* Adapted from R. Cross, A. Parker, and S. P. Borgatti, *A Bird's-Eye View: Using Social Network Analysis to Improve Knowledge Creation and Sharing* (Somers, NY: IBM Institute for Business Values, 2002). Used with permission.

The Principles of Public Engagement

Social networks have burgeoned within the public sphere with the rise in popularity of participatory democracy. Complementing representative democratic systems, participatory democracy or public engagement seeks to place decision making into the hands of ordinary citizens. Rousseau, for example, believed that civic participation in decision making would increase the feelings among individuals that they truly belong to the community in which they live.

There is no specific methodology that can be used to facilitate every occurrence of public engagement, since each context contains its own unique mix of people, issues, and institutions. Nevertheless, bolstered by the active involvement of such public interest organizations as the National Coalition for Dialogue and Deliberation, the Co-Intelligence Institute, the Center for Wise Democracy, and AmericaSpeaks, a set of principles[28] have been derived for engaging citizens in effective collaborative action. These seven core principles serve as guidelines for building mutual understanding and working toward caring and productive decision making within most social networks, even among those not necessarily working in the public sphere.

These principles are defined as follows:

1. *Planning and preparation:* Plan, design, and convene the engagement specifically to serve the purpose of the effort and the needs of the participants
2. *Inclusion and diversity:* Incorporate diverse voices, ideas, and information to lay the groundwork for quality outcomes and democratic legitimacy
3. *Collaboration and shared purpose:* Support organizers, participants, and implementers to sustain efforts on behalf of the common good
4. *Listening and learning:* Help participants listen, explore, and learn without predetermining outcomes

---

[28] The Core Principles of Public Engagement (Version 3.0) were developed by members of leading public engagement organizations. They are posted on the website of the Coalition for Dialogue and Deliberation at: *www.thataway.org/2009/pep_project/*. Retrieved December 21, 2009.

5. *Transparency and trust:* Promote openness, especially by providing a public record of the people, resources, forums, and outcomes involved
6. *Impact and action:* Ensure that the engagement has real potential to make a difference
7. *Sustained participation and democratic culture:* Build a culture of participation among associated programs and institutions that support quality public engagement

ACTIVITY 5.7

The Seven Core Principles for Effective Public Engagement

The seven principles are overlapping and mutually reinforcing. This activity assists network participants in developing criteria for evaluating the quality of their network decision making in terms of participation and involvement. What is suggested is that the more the reliance on these principles, the more likely will be a sense of leaderful engagement; the less reliance on them, the less likely will be the feeling of leaderful engagement. Thus, there are explicit steps to be taken in encouraging their wider use as well as steps to be taken to point out the traps to be avoided.

STEP 1: Familiarize yourself with the seven principles to building authentic engagement within the social networks in which you are serving in a weaver capacity. *Public engagement* is meant here to entail the convening of diverse yet representative groups of people who engage with one another on a variety of viewpoints in conversations that are well facilitated and that provide important guidance to decisions to be made by one another, by policymakers, or by fellow citizens.

STEP 2: Assemble as many of your network participants as you deem feasible and most useful. If your network isn't too large, perhaps you can assemble the full network membership as it currently stands. The intent of this step is to determine when and how these principles have been restricted. Once these behaviors have been identified, as a team you can list them as practices that you would ask that members do *less* of. In Figure 5.3, below each principle are some suggested practices in which members are currently or prospectively engaging that would fall under this categorization. Your assignment together is to review the relevance of the listed practices, add your own items, and communicate them throughout the network.

FIGURE **5.3**

Practices to Be Avoided in Public Engagement

We ask that members of the network consider doing *less* of the following:

In Planning and Preparation

- Relevant stakeholders are not involved.
- The convening schedule is inflexible or rushed.
- There is inadequate time to do what needs to be done.
- Logistical, class, racial, or cultural barriers are left unaddressed.

[List your own]

In Inclusion and Diversity

- Participants have little chance to speak out or are unheard.
- Some stakeholders feel their interests are suppressed or ignored.
- There is only token diversity present.
- Information that is presented is biased or designed to move people in a specific direction.

[List your own]

In Collaboration and Shared Purpose

- Power holders deliver one-way pronouncements.
- Conversations are stilted or stifled.
- Experts present with "all the answers."
- The important or relevant decisions have already been made, in the back room.

[List your own]

In Listening and Learning

- Communication consists of going through the motions and then announcing a predetermined outcome.
- Assertive, mainstream, and official voices dominate.
- Available information is biased, scanty, or inaccessible.

(Continued on next page)

FIGURE **5.3**   *(Continued)*

- Lack of time or inflexibility of the process makes it impossible to deal with the complexity of the issue.

[List your own]

In Transparency and Trust

- It is hard to find out who is involved, what happened, and why.
- There is concern about hidden agendas and ethics.
- Participants suspect the facilitators have hidden motives.
- Participants are not comfortable being open about their own thoughts and feelings.

[List your own]

In Impact and Action

- Participants have little sense of having any effect—before, during, or after the engagement.
- There is no follow-through, so few people seem to know what happened.
- Findings and recommendations are inarticulate, ill timed, or ignored.
- Any energy catalyzed by the event quickly dies out.

[List your own]

In Sustained Engagement and Democratic Culture

- The engagement is a one-off event, isolated from the ongoing life of the network.
- Behind-the-scenes maneuvering still dominates as the key interactions.
- Few people have any expectation that authentic or empowered participation is possible.
- Privileged people dominate, undermining the ability of those who are marginalized to participate.

[List your own]

STEP 3: Continuing with your assembled membership, determine when and how the principles of public engagement have been promoted. As a team, list what you would like members to do *more* of (or at least continue to do). So, in Figure 5.4, following each principle are some suggested practices in which members are currently or prospectively engaging that would fall under this, now more positive, categorization. Your assignment together is to review the relevance of these listed practices, add your own items, and communicate them throughout the network.

. . . .

FIGURE **5.4**

Practices to Be Promoted in Public Engagement

We ask that members of the network consider doing *more* of the following:

In Planning and Preparation

- All stakeholders, conveners, and experts engage together in planning and organizing the network.
- Hospitable, accessible, and functional environments are created for all convenings.
- Adequate support and facilitation is provided.
- Participants are clear on the unique context, purpose, and task at hand.
- [List your own]

In Inclusion and Diversity

- There is demographic diversity and diversity of views on the issue at hand.
- There is opportunity to consider alternative perspectives representing different "sides" of the issue.
- Participants feel respected; their views are welcomed, heard, and responded to.
- Special efforts are made to enable otherwise marginalized or silent voices to meaningfully engage.
- [List your own]

(Continued on next page)

FIGURE **5.4** *(Continued)*

In Collaboration and Shared Purpose

- Differences are explored rather than ignored, allowing a shared sense of a desired future to emerge.
- People with different backgrounds and ideologies work together on every aspect of the engagement.
- All interested parties are considered equal participants in the conversations.
- Participants share agreed-upon outcomes and action steps.
- [List your own]

In Listening and Learning

- Skilled neutral facilitators and guidelines encourage participatory sharing of views.
- Participants listen and are curious to learn things about themselves, about others, and about the issues before them.
- Shared intention and powerful questions guide participants' explorations, including their disagreements.
- There is an appropriate balance between consulting facts and considering participants' experience, values, and emotions.
- [List your own]

In Transparency and Trust

- Relevant information is shared in a timely way, respecting privacy where necessary.
- Participants can easily access information and get and stay involved.
- Those with official roles or expertise are straightforward, concerned, and answerable.
- Public records are made available on those involved and about agreed-upon outcomes.
- [List your own]

(Continued on next page)

··

FIGURE **5.4**   *(Continued)*

In Impact and Action

- There is evidence to make people believe their engagement was meaningful.
- Communications ensure that diverse and affected stakeholders know about the engagement.
- The effort is linked to other efforts on the issue being addressed.
- The engagement results in communities becoming more vibrant and successful.
- [List your own]

In Sustained Engagement and Democratic Culture

- Being linked to related engagement practices, democratic participation increasingly becomes an embedded standard practice.
- Participants gain knowledge and skills in democratic methods.
- Participants and others involved develop a sense of ownership and buy-in.
- Relationships and spaces are built to support ongoing quality public engagement.
- [List your own]

··

STEP 4: Having produced lists of what the network would like to see members do *less* and *more* of, the full community should now engage in a full dialogue on learning. Especially if a subgroup from the network was assembled to work on the lists, it is critical that there be outreach to other nodes or stakeholders to ensure that the guidelines become a product of the full network and are subsequently endorsed as a communitywide endeavor.

Here are some processes to use along these lines:

1. Publish throughout your network the principles of public engagement as well as both sets of practices from Figures 5.3 and 5.4. Your final lists will be those generated by your workgroup, not necessarily those originally listed in the figures.

2. Ask for commentary, changes, and overall recommendations and give members a deadline for their input.

3. After obtaining feedback from Step 2, disseminate the revised lists but ask that they be considered living practices that can be altered as conditions change within the network, such as growth or decline, changing membership, new responsibilities, funding priorities, and the like.

4. Suggest that clusters within the network assemble both online and face to face to work through these principles and guidelines to see if their application might benefit network effectiveness.

5. Continue to publish real-time experiences working with these documents, which, in turn, might lead to changes in the network's mission and operating practices.

CASE STUDY

Network Weaving:
Redesigning an Annual Conference to Strengthen a
Community of Practice

Rosa Zubizarreta and Bruce Nayowith

Setting and Characters

Our weaving role began when we were asked to support the redesign of an upcoming conference for a loose-knit community of practice, to which we the writers belong, within the realm of applied psychology. This community consists of professionals and lay people who have been trained in a particular mind-body practice, many of whom gather together annually at this conference, sponsored by a different host within a different country each year.

Prior to the intervention, the main form of network connection, outside the annual conference, was a single e-mail list that was hosted by the central training organization. While many people within this community were applying the mind-body practice in a wide variety of fields, there was often little knowledge of one another's work and most was being carried out individually. That year's conference host was seeking to help the community grow and differentiate by developing stronger internal networks of collaborative working relationships, and asked us to assist him in this effort.

In prior years, the annual conference had been organized in fairly traditional ways, consisting of various presentations and workshops offered by community members. Conference participants, however, would organize informal networking activities amongst themselves, yet these activities would take place for brief periods of time and on the "fringes" of the main conference schedule. That year, the host's plan was to allocate an entire preconference day for participants so that they could explore potential collaborations and strengthen their respective nodal roles within the emerging networks. The ultimate purpose of the plan was to develop the community's shared knowledge base by expanding and deepening the various applications of the basic mind-body process that this community of practice held in common.

Our Formal "Entry" into the Process

To make fuller use of the valuable face-to-face time at the conference, the host wanted the "weaving" process to begin well in advance. He invited us to support him in this work. The initial idea was to create a new e-mail list for the people who had registered for the conference and to invite participants to communicate with one another and begin to self-organize into interest groups. We were asked to serve as list facilitators, offering any assistance that was needed to support the emergence of these interest-based networks.

As part of our entry into this project, we paid attention to some of the items included under "Membership and Purpose" in Activity 5.4 of this fieldbook (as we did for our interventions in many other instances) and planned for the new network's ongoing evaluation. In particular, we wanted to make sure we had a clear picture of the conference host's desired outcomes, as he was the initiating "co-weaver" of this project. At the same time, we wanted to explore his commitment to the open-ended nature of a self-organizing process and his willingness to course-correct as needed, depending on the participants' needs and the project's evolving character. As part of these beginning conversations, we agreed to periodically revisit our initial plans so that we could adapt them to the network members' needs.

We also committed to an ethic of transparency, sharing our process with the conference host and participants to ensure that everyone felt fully comfortable with our proposed and ongoing interventions.

Our Community Invitation

Once the new e-mail list was formed, we turned our attention to the new network's structure. The conference host sent out an invitation describing the initial vision and purpose for the preconference day and introducing us as list facilitators. In turn, we invited participants to share their ideas for the kind of interest group they might want to form. Most significantly, we encouraged particular individuals to consider becoming "interest group hosts"—a catalytic hub role for an emerging interest group. This would involve becoming the "point person" whom others could contact. We had earlier identified this as one of the key functions that would help these networks accomplish their purpose.

A related aspect of the interest group host's role was supporting ongoing communications among the members of that emerging group. Once a group began to form, they would be encouraged to move their internal communications "off-list," in order to keep traffic on the preconference e-mail list more manageable. We wanted to avoid any potential bottlenecks that might occur if all of the internal communications within the emerging network groups took place on this one list.

As people began to step forward as hosts, we realized that it would be helpful for us to periodically send out messages to the preconference list, with summaries of the various interest groups that were forming to date, along with contact information for each host. That way, people who were still looking for a group to join would not have to wade through old posts to find what they needed; they would be able to more easily access information about emerging interest groups and their domains.

As weavers, we saw our role as supporting the emerging interest group hosts, who themselves would become weavers of their own networks, and we made ourselves available to them by phone and online. At the same time, we realized that there was a need to continue to emphasize the original vision, both in our direct contact with the emerging weavers as well as in our periodic posts to the new list. We made a point to remind people that the purpose of these new interest group networks was for everyone to have an opportunity to participate in a leaderful fashion. Members would not, for example, simply represent a captive audience for hosts to present their own work. Rather, if people in an interest group agreed, they might take turns utilizing the group forum as a sounding board for their own projects.

Ways in Which Reality Began to Differ from the Original Plan

As the network weaving process evolved, several areas of divergence from our initial intentions became apparent. For one thing, the conference host's initial vision had been of small groups that would be working fairly intensively on their area of interest, meeting several times during the introductory evening and following day that had been set aside for this work. However, while people were excited about the opportunity to meet in groups and began communicating directly with one another around their shared interests, many of the participants expressed a desire to join more than one network out of sheer interest in the diverse subject matter.

We also found that while several groups began to coalesce, a significant number of people who registered for the conference did *not* want to commit to an interest group ahead of time; instead they wanted to wait until they arrived at the conference itself. In the spirit of course correction, we discussed these developments with the conference host, who agreed with us that we needed to be flexible in order to meet people's needs and interests. We came up with a "both-and" response, restating the intention and purpose behind the original idea (offering people enough time to engage in in-depth work on particular applications) while at the same time acknowledging that some people might prefer to participate in various network groups. In addition, we suggested that anyone who wanted to participate in two or more groups begin communicating with the various networks they wanted to be a part of to see how their respective meeting schedules were evolving and what kinds of arrangements could be worked out.

The conference host also decided to redesign the introductory evening so that people who had not yet joined a group would have the opportunity to do so then. A "parallel track" was established for anyone who did not wish to join any interest group but simply wanted to spend time in shared practice.

Another unexpected yet welcomed development was that people began using the new preconference list for other forms of conference-related networking, such as coordinating travel arrangements with one another. All of these various preconference communications began to generate an unprecedented "buzz" well in advance of the conference itself.

Outcomes

Both short-term and long-term outcomes for this networking project were deemed to be very successful. In their feedback at the end of the conference, participants conveyed that the networking groups had been one of the highlights of the conference. One notable feature of the groups was the variety of formats: some groups had met once, others twice, and several more frequently. They also ranged in size. While the conference host's initial proposal had been to have larger groups subdivide into working group size (four to six members), some of the groups that formed initially were fairly large (twenty-plus members) and chose to remain that way. The larger size gave them a certain level of resilience and diversity. On the other hand, some of the more refined topics drew fewer people, yet their participants were equally enthusiastic about their experience.

During the introductory evening event dedicated to organizing the network project, people had been encouraged to think about how they might continue to work together beyond the time of the conference itself. As it turned out, several of the groups did in fact continue to meet online and through phone conferencing.

Other new and more specialized networks have also emerged. Many of these groups have created their own websites to post information about their ongoing work. Over the past five years, a few of the networks have developed such strong ties that they have begun to host their own annual conferences, focusing more specifically on their respective fields of application.

That first year, there was so much enthusiasm for this network-weaving effort that the organizers for the following year's general conference decided to implement a similar plan, designating time during the conference for interest groups to meet, and producing a preconference e-mail list to "get the ball rolling." And, we were invited to return to support those efforts, though of late, due to other commitments we are no longer as directly involved. But our community's network development goes on.

Afterword

Having experimented with many of the activities presented in this fieldbook, I hope that my readers and users can now join together to bring leaderful practice into full fruition. For so many years, people have voiced a concern whether the noble aspirations of a democracy applied to corporate and organizational life can ever be actualized. People understand the value of maintaining an ethic of fair participation and humility in decision making. Everybody's contribution would be valued, and people would recognize how much they need to count on others to get things done. They would see their role in leadership as serving others, not seeking power for its own sake. When these democratic principles are engaged, it is no wonder that they can be harnessed to contribute to the productiveness and growth of communities and organizations.

But leaderful practice has in some sectors remained no more than an aspiration; as we admitted at the outset, in many of our cultures it is not a quality that is standing by ready to be adopted. It needs to be developed. People in organizations need to evolve both an appreciation for and an ability to adopt leaderful practice. In some fortunate circumstances, long-standing traditions may have been set in motion to mobilize the community to learn as it grows. In most other circumstances, we likely need particular individuals to emerge to serve as agents of change. And this is where this fieldbook takes over—to help all of you serving as change agents of leaderful practice do your noble work with as much success and satisfaction as you and your clients deserve.

Using the activities and cases illustrated in this fieldbook, change agents—be they internal or external to the system in question—can work closely with their clients to transform both self and other to become more cognitively receptive and then more behaviorally confident in effecting leaderful behavior. The coverage in this book has started at the level of the individual. I started here to help individuals understand the tension between their aspirations and their current reality. The view taken was that once we understand our own struggles, then we can begin to see their embeddedness in the reality around us in our social world.

The activities at the individual level were designed to assist coaches' work with their clients to achieve the latters' personal learning goals and to produce greater self-efficacy along with heightened states of autonomy, meaning, and responsibility. Coaching can help people explore the social, political, and even emotional reactions that might be blocking their own operating effectiveness. Otherwise delicate issues—whether conflicts of interest, working relationships with other peers, or an individual's own growth and development—can be given a forum for open consideration. Once one masters a sense of personal freedom, one can begin to model both self-leadership and collective leadership.

The interpersonal level of experience focuses on the process of uncovering our own identity and wisdom through the eyes of others. This process is unveiled largely through dialogue, which entails not just an advocacy of our own views but a deep inquiry into the views, values, and feelings of others. The coaching activities used at the interpersonal level help the engaged parties surface the often undiscussable assumptions that impede their mutual understanding. Once they agree on the meaning of their mutual work, they can learn to work together on their collective projects.

We have described change agency at the team level as one of facilitation. Facilitators, often by example as much as by explanation, share their knowledge of group dynamics so that members of a team realize the challenge but also the benefits of developing their team. In time, these members can assume the necessary roles to manage themselves. The activities in the team-level chapter were designed to provide teams with the reflective practices necessary for critical self-renewal.

We depicted the change agent at the organizational level as the classic OD (organizational development) consultant, trained to encourage the endorsement of a leaderful culture that values learning and democratic participation. Acknowledging the powerful influence of culture, OD consultants share with their clients how cultural artifacts can shape cultural norms. In the leaderful tradition, we are interested in conditions to create a culture of learning where it becomes acceptable to dialogue openly about otherwise undiscussable topics. The activities in this chapter were designed to create such cultures that tolerate dissent and maximize full commitment and participation.

The social network level of experience discloses the reality of social life in the post-bureaucratic era—we live in a networked economy characterized by webs of partnerships. It is rare to be able to accomplish most ventures without collaborative practices in which stakeholders learn to nurture connections and share resources. The title we have given to the change agent who not only helps to create new networks but also helps to sustain them once formed is the "weaver." The activities in the social network chapter were designed to help the weaver establish a relationship among stakeholders based on the development of social capital, citizenship, and trust rather than on rules and regulations.

Although no longer a strange idea nor one that hasn't seen exemplars and applications, leaderful practice requires the push of agency to become an everyday reality. We can create our own reality, but we have to engage with others. It is through such involvement that we may achieve a moral democratic order. But as John Dewey reminded us, we need to possess a sense of civility in which our self-interest would be sacrificed for the common good. And the common good would not evolve from altruism; it would not entail an extension of self *for* others, but rather *with* others.

So, people in their collective endeavors by acting together in the world can shape their local communities for the better, that is, in ways that are more responsive to their mutual needs. It has become too easy to fold our tents around the hierarchical principle of organizational behavior. So, let us begin, simply but unequivocally, in the day-to-day behaviors that we people of goodwill may extend to one another. Everyone can be a party to leadership. Everyone can value another's interest. In due course, we may also take it as natural to enlist our partners to forge a leaderful identity.

About the Author

JOSEPH A. RAELIN IS AN INTERNATIONAL AUTHORITY in collaborative leadership development and work-based learning. He holds the Asa S. Knowles Chair of Practice-Oriented Education at Northeastern University and is also a professor in the College of Business Administration. He was formerly professor of management at the Wallace E. Carroll School of Management at Boston College. He received his Ph.D. from the State University of New York at Buffalo. His research has centered on human resource development, focusing in particular on executive and management education through the use of action learning. Joe is a prolific writer with over 100 articles appearing in the leading management journals and the author of seven books. Among the latter are: *The Clash of Cultures: Managers Managing Professionals*, considered now to be a classic in the field of professionals and bureaucracy (Harvard Business School Press, 1991); *Creating Leaderful Organizations: How to Bring Out Leadership in Everyone* (Berrett-Koehler, 2003); and the latest edition of *Work-Based Learning: Bridging Knowledge and Action in the Workplace* (Jossey-Bass, 2008).

Joe is also a management consultant with thirty-five years of experience working with a wide variety of organizational clients. Among his many honors, he received the 2010 David Bradford Outstanding Educator Award from the OBTS Teaching Society for Management Educators. What intrigues him is the profound transition in leadership development that occurs when we think of leadership not as a set of traits to be found in individuals but as the activities of groups of practitioners working together on a collective practice. So, he likes to think of himself as part of a new movement called "leadership-as-practice," and is frankly more interested in leadership than leaders. Thought about in this way, leaderful development, as depicted in this fieldbook, will be more about what we can do as change agents to develop leadership in our multiple communities than to augment the heroic traits of any one person.

Quoting from the afterword of this book, Joe wishes that his readers begin their leaderful journey "… simply but unequivocally in the day-to-day consideration that they as people of good will extend to one another. Everyone can be a party to leadership. In due course, we may take it as natural to enlist our partners to forge a leaderful identity."

About the Contributors

John Foster is head of talent and organization for IDEO, where he applies the IDEO design process internally to help the firm stay at the leading edge of design and innovation consulting. He has a deep background in organization development, leadership development, and instructional design, with experience working inside Fidelity Investments, Levi Strauss, and Mercury Interactive (now part of HP). Prior to his internal corporate roles, he was a leadership and team-building facilitator for Pecos River Learning Centers, where he worked with dozens of Fortune 500 companies on team performance and organizational change initiatives.

John began his career as a program director with the YMCA, working in summer camping programs, outdoor education, and outdoor leadership programs. He earned a master's degree in education from Colorado State University and holds a twin B.A. in psychology and communications from Miami University. He lives in California with his wife and four children and enjoys travelling, playing guitar, and outdoor adventure sports.

Victoria J. Marsick, Ph.D. is co-director with Martha Gephart of the J.M. Huber Institute for Learning in Organizations at Teachers College, Columbia University, where she is a professor of adult & organizational learning in the Department of Organization and Leadership. She holds a Ph.D. in adult education from the University of California, Berkeley, and an M.P.A. in international public administration from Syracuse University. Victoria is a principal in Partners for Learning and Leadership. Her consulting practice is focused on action and strategic learning. Victoria's scholarly interests include informal and incidental learning at the individual, team, and organizational levels; action learning; and organizational learning assessment.

Judy O'Neil, Ed.D. is president of the consulting firm, Partners for Learning and Leadership, Inc., which specializes in action technologies including action learning. She holds an Ed.D. and M.A. in adult education from Teachers College, Columbia University, New York and is on the adjunct faculty at Teachers College. She spent thirty years in the corporate world specializing in human resource development and organizational change. Her clients have included Covidien, the Government of Bermuda, VNU (Nielsen Media Ratings), Berlex Pharmaceuticals, AstraZeneca Pharmaceuticals, Fidelity Investments, PSE&G, RR Donnelley, AT&T, Ernst and Young, Norwest, The Mount Sinai Medical Center of New York, New York Transit Authority, and The Hartford Insurance.

Karen E. Watkins, Ph.D. is professor of Human Resource and Organizational Development in the College of Education at The University of Georgia. She holds a Ph.D. in education administration from the University of Texas at Austin and an M.A. in English from the University of Wisconsin, Madison. Karen is a principal in Partners for Learning and Leadership. Her consulting practice is based on action learning and evaluating management learning. Karen's scholarly interests include incidental learning, action science, and organizational learning assessment. Watkins and Marsick developed and validated the Dimensions of the Learning Organization Questionnaire used in over seventy published studies. Named Scholar of the Year by the Academy of Human Resource Development and a distinguished graduate by The University of Texas at Austin, Community College Leadership Program, she was inducted into the International Adult and Continuing Education Hall of Fame in 2003.

Philip McArthur, Ed.D. is a partner and cofounder of Action Design, a consulting firm specializing in organizational learning and professional development. He holds a master's and doctorate in counseling and consulting psychology from Harvard University, and trained as a family therapist at the Family Institute of Cambridge. He has had over twenty years of experience as an executive and team coach, and he conducts professional development workshops on creating productive conversations and building effective relationships in organizations. His clients include nonprofits as well as companies in a broad range of industries including pharmaceuticals, financial services, information technology, manufacturing and consulting.

Leonard J. Glick is an executive professor of management and organizational development in the College of Business Administration of Northeastern University. Prior to joining the faculty at Northeastern, Professor Glick had nearly twenty years of experience as both an external and internal organizational effectiveness consultant. His experience and expertise include the design and implementation of high performance work systems, organizational culture, self-managing teams, organizational change, and non-stop learning ("How to Decrease Training and Increase Learning"). Among the courses he teaches are: High Commitment Organizations, Great Companies, Strategic Human Resource Management, and Organizational Behavior.

Rosa Zubizarreta consults with small business and non-profit organizations, facilitating creative collaboration and practicing collaborative therapy with individuals and families. She holds an M.A. in psychology from the Organization Development program at Sonoma State University, an M.S.W. from Springfield College, and an M.A. in Multicultural Education from University of San Francisco. Her expertise and experience include helping people transform conflict into co-creativity, facilitating co-intelligence in task groups, and supporting participatory work re-design processes.

Bruce Nayowith is a practicing emergency physician in western Massachusetts. He received his M.D. from Jefferson Medical College in 1978, and has worked for the Indian Health Service in the U.S. and with the Catholic Church in Chiapas, Mexico. He has led internal efforts for quality improvement in various health organizations, and he pursues an interest in systems and processes that encourage optimum unfolding of individual and systemic potential, including Focusing and Dynamic Facilitation.